For Richer, For Poorer

An Investigation of the Irish Pension System

Recent **tasc** *publications*

An Outburst of Frankness: Community Arts in Ireland – A Reader ed. by Sandy Fitzgerald, Tasc at New Island, 2004.

Selling Out? Privatisation in Ireland by Paul Sweeney, Tasc at New Island, 2004.

After the Ball by Fintan O Toole, Tasc at New Island, 2003.

For Richer, For Poorer

An Investigation of the Irish Pension System

Jim Stewart (*Editor*)

For Richer, For Poorer
First published 2005
by tasc at New Island
an imprint of New Island Press
2 Brookside
Dundrum Road
Dublin 14

www.newisland.ie

ISBN 1-904301 89 4.

Typeset by Ashfield Press
Cover design by Public Communications Centre

Printed in Ireland by
Betaprint Limited, Dublin

Contents

tasc in 2004, commissioned the contributors to undertake an analysis of the Irish pension system and the principal issues facing it. The **tasc** agenda is to foster new thinking and public understanding of ways to create a more equal society. The members of the research group were asked to pay particular attention to the impact of the current pension system on the level of inequality in Irish society and to consider alternatives. This book is the outcome of their work.

Earlier drafts of the papers in this book were presented at a seminar given jointly by the Pension Policy Research Group* and **tasc** on September 23, 2004. We are especially indebted to the participants for their very helpful comments and criticisms on the day. Needless to say, not all participants agree with the views of the authors, which remain their responsibility alone.

Contributors

Peter Connell	works in Information Services, Trinity College Dublin and has a particular interest in population projections.
Gerard Hughes	works in the Economic and Social Research Institute, Dublin and has written extensively on pension issues.
Anthony McCashin	works in the Department of Social Studies, Trinity College Dublin and has written extensively on the Irish Social Security System.
Jim Stewart	works in the School of Business Studies, Trinity College Dublin and has written several papers on financial aspects of pension systems.
Sue Ward	has published extensively on the UK pension system and was a member of the UK pensions regulatory body.

* All the contributors (with the exception of Sue Ward) are members of the Pension Policy Research Group based in Trinity College Dublin.

www.tascnet.ie

Chapter 1

Issues in Pension Provision

BY JIM STEWART

1.1 INTRODUCTION: PERMANENT AND PENSION-ABLE?

In a young society like Ireland's, most people prefer not to think about pensions. It is not just that the issue is one for the long-term, but also that the subject itself reminds us that, in the long-term, we are all dead. In a fast-changing, energetic country, the future often seems so utterly unpredictable that there is no point in thinking about it. The term 'permanent and pensionable', once the essence of everything that parents desired for their children, is now, in common usage, the epitome of boredom.

But while it may well be true that there is something odd about a 22 year-old who worries about his or her pension, it is just as true that there is something odd about a society that doesn't think seriously about the issue. The fear of penury in old age has haunted people for millennia, and the development of systems to ensure a dignified retirement is one of the great achievements of developed societies in the first half of the 20th century. The introduction of the State old age pension in 1909 in Ireland and the UK had an enormously positive effect on the lives of millions, lifting the dread of ending one's days without dignity in a Poor Law Workhouse. The very fact that pensions have become a dull subject, so taken for granted that they are not really worth discussing, is a mark of the difference they have made to the lives of so many. Yet that mark of civilisation is now a mark of danger. Pensions can't be taken for granted any more.

One of the reasons for this is precisely that life has improved for the majority of people. People in countries like Ireland live longer. Rising life expectancy should be good news, in particular as evidence from other countries shows it is associated with reduced levels of ill health. In public policy circles, however, this good news is often discussed in the context of the 'population time bomb', meaning that it will become ever more difficult to provide income to a growing proportion of retired persons in the population.

As well as the projected increase in the number of people aged over 65, we have to deal with the large number of those aged under 65 who are not members of an occupational pension. This means that on retirement they will be dependent on State sources of pension income. But State pension payments are at a low level, relative to the income of those in employment. There is, consequently, a real risk of poverty amongst the retired population. How, then, can we avoid a future in which more and more people are dependent on an income from the State which keeps their heads above water but leaves them in relative poverty, with all the attendant problems of inequality, isolation and lack of access to the good things that society has to offer?

One widely advocated solution is to increase reliance on private sector pension provision. This would mean, for example, that as the number of those aged over 65 increased, State old age pension payments would not increase in the same proportion. For obvious reasons, the private pensions industry favours this solution. But others, including the Pensions Board (which is the main regulator of the pensions industry in Ireland), also support an increasing reliance on privately funded schemes. By and large, it has been accepted that the future lies with private pensions.

Increased reliance on private sector provision raises a number of issues, however. Pension policies are necessarily complex. They are made even more complex because the returns they generate (and the risks they entail) are often connected to aspects of the tax system. For this reason, they are subject to extensive regulation (by, for example, the Pensions Board). However, it is difficult for individuals to obtain independent advice on pension products or, indeed, pension entitlements. Private sector institutions, of their nature, provide financial products, including pensions, for profit. This may result in a conflict of   interest where selling a pension policy generates commission but giving unbiased advice does not. However hard they try to act with integrity, pension advisors who work for financial institutions are vendors first, and advisors second.

In this book, we provide an analysis of the way the benefits of current pension arrangements are skewed towards the better off, i.e. those who can afford or benefit from private occupational pension provision. We show how the current system has evolved to serve the interests of the pension industry to the detriment of the vast majority of current and prospective pensioners. Our aim is to offer a critical evaluation of this system and to make policy recommendations, which will prevent the present income inequalities of pensioners being locked in to future arrangements. The book's message is less about the overall inadequacy in pension provision and more about the way pensions are currently widening income inequality in Irish society and leaving a large proportion of pensioners (particularly women) without adequate income in their old age.

In essence, we demonstrate that: -

- The current pension system serves to increase inequality by redistributing state resources away from more vulnerable sections of the Irish population (i.e. those entirely dependent on the State pension) and towards the better off (i.e. those who can gain tax relief from contributions to funded pension schemes).

- The delivery of pensions to those with atypical work patterns is seriously inadequate. Women are especially badly affected because they may have long periods out of the (paid) labour force and are more likely to work part-time. Those who change jobs frequently, as in the building industry, or have low pay are also poorly served by the current pension system.

- The interests of the pensions industry have skewed State policy towards an emphasis on funding pensions by, for example, extensive tax reliefs and the promotion of individual pension products such as Additional Voluntary Contributions (AVCs) and Personal Retirement Savings Accounts (PRSAs). We question the efficiency and effectiveness of these systems that rely on private provision. Costs in the pensions industry are high. The pensions industry is large and dependent on highly paid professionals. Yet survey evidence shows that most income of retired persons comes from the State old age pension.

Against this background, we set out the criteria that should underlie pensions policy in Ireland and make a series of key proposals on what should constitute a pension strategy.

In Ireland there are three main ways in which pension income is paid: -

1. The State pension. State payments come in two forms. Those who have made sufficient social

insurance payments get the old age contributory pension. Those who are not qualified for such a pension get the less valuable old age non-contributory pension.

2. The occupational pension. This results from membership of a pension scheme organised by an employer. But only certain types of employment tend to result in an occupational pension, for example a permanent job in the State or semi-state sector, or in large organisations such as the main banks.

3. Individual pension arrangements such as Additional Voluntary Contributions (AVCs) or, in future, Personal Retirement Savings Accounts (PRSAs). Individual pension arrangements could be supplementary to an occupational pension, or the main source of pension income.

Many people, in addition, may also have some investment income although income from this source may be low. Finally, some may continue to work past the general retirement age of 65, a situation, more generally, which is increasingly advocated as a partial solution to the future cost of pension provision. Pension income could come from a number of these sources. For most people there is a ceiling on the level of pension income so that a State old age contributory pension, when combined with an occupational pension, cannot exceed two-thirds of pre retirement income adjusted for any increased pay levels from the date of retirement.

It may seem obvious that the purpose of a pension system is to provide retirement income. Apart from the fact that the system sometimes seems to be run in order to give secure employment to those in the pensions industry, though, it is in fact used for a wider variety of purposes. The pension system is expected to perform many other purposes, for example to fund early retirement, or to reward key employees or groups with higher pension payments than is merited by their contributions or years of work (by, for instance, giving added years). Some have even argued that the pension system should be used to develop an active market in long-term sources of finance to encourage investment, and in particular to increase the flow of funds to small firms[1]. It is also used as an effective means of reducing income taxation for high-income earners and, for some, the pension system has become an important part of tax planning/tax avoidance. For this reason, pension contributions may constitute the largest component of pay to senior executives.

1.2 SUMMARY OF BOOK

We begin by considering evidence on the relative importance of different sources of pension income to those aged over 65. In Chapter 2, Jim Stewart shows that a majority of those aged over 65 are dependent solely on the State old age pension. This is especially so for women, who tend to live longer. This heavy dependency on the State pension raises significant questions about the ability of private sector pension provision to serve the needs of such people and to provide them with future pension income in a fair and efficient way. It is difficult to see current pension policies, with their emphasis on complex financial products and tax relief as an incentive, providing a major source of future retirement income for this very large section of the older population.

It is widely recognised that there are many issues relating to the future of pension systems but among the most important is the possibility of a population 'time bomb' – a growing proportion of elderly in the population, whose future incomes cannot be sustained at current levels and retirement patterns. In Chapter 3, Peter Connell examines this issue and considers in particular the effects of migration and increased longevity. The key point he makes is that population forecasting is uncertain, particularly over a long time period (50 years). For Ireland in particular, the biggest source of uncertainty is the level of in-migration. But it is easier to forecast the number of those aged 65+ over a 20- year period, because very few migrants tend to be over 45. This means that we can be quite certain that there will be an increase in the numbers aged over 65, but there is greater uncertainty in forecasting the relative proportion of those aged 65+ in the population as a whole, the so-called old-age dependency ratio.

How will the pensions of this growing section of the population be funded? The official view is that the answer lies in increased saving via funded pensions and managed funds in the private sector. It is further argued that a private sector funded pension system has other advantages in terms of increasing savings rates and economy wide invest-ment and the efficiency with which capital is invested, thus increasing economic growth and further facilitating the payment of pensions. These beneficial effects on capital markets have been advanced by the Pensions Board (1998, p. 95) as major reasons for increased use of private schemes. But what was not emphasised in the report by the Pensions Board (1998) is that there may also be negative effects on capital markets resulting from pension fund activities. In Chapter 4, Jim Stewart raises critical questions about the growth of funded pensions, in terms of risk and costs. This chapter also examines other possible ways to fill the gap between what is needed to provide a funded pension and what is projected to be available.

The State old age pension system is a mandatory pensions system, which forms part of the overall social security system. The Pensions Board has set as a desirable target the goal that a social welfare pension should pay out 34 per cent of average industrial earnings (Pensions Board,

1998, p. 87). This is not high in comparison with other EU countries and it is not clear why 34 per cent should be seen as a desirable number. One reason, as argued by employers, is undoubtedly the increased costs of funding pensions and the possible effects on competitiveness (Pensions Board, 1998, pp. 88 and 101). The Pensions Board proposed that any increase in pension payments beyond this 34 per cent level will come from privately-funded sources. One difficulty which arises is that while many occupational schemes are mandatory (employees are required to become members) some schemes are not and individual provision is voluntary. Membership of private sector pension schemes is particularly low for those with atypical working careers (part-time workers, those with periods out of the workforce, and those with frequent changes in employ-ment). This gives rise to issues of low coverage for private sector schemes, particularly amongst certain occupational groups and age profiles, including women with dependent children.

Considerable energy and effort has been expended on private sector solutions to low coverage, such as PRSAs. More recently, it has been argued that there should be much greater emphasis on persuasion, for example through the school education system and the provision of pension plans for children, and the possibility of making private sector pension provision compulsory has been discussed (Pensions Board, 1998, pp. 130-1).

Given, however, that the State social security system is currently the main source of income to retired persons in Ireland and the difficulties with funded pension schemes such as the recent low or negative stock market returns, social security based pensions are likely to retain their significance. But questions have been raised as to the sustainability of the State social welfare pension. It has been argued that the State social security system is relatively more expensive than the private alternatives. This raises issues as to what is the proper role for the State social security system in a market economy. In Chapter 5, Anthony McCashin considers this issue in an Irish context in terms of efficiency and equity, and argues that a key reform should be the introduction of a basic universal income for retired persons. A strategy along these lines might create a 'basic pension' for all citizens above a certain age, untaxed and without a means test. Occupational pensions would be integrated with the 'basic pension' and the cost would be partly offset by a significant curtailment of the tax incentives for occupational pensions, PRSAs and Approved Retirement Funds.

One aspect of the private pension schemes that is seldom alluded to is that they are not really private at all. The State subsidises them to a very significant extent through tax reliefs. Although never quantified, it is likely that a significant component of pension fund returns derive from their tax-free status. The mirror side of tax-free status for pension funds and contributions is that tax expenditures associated with pension provision are large and growing. In Chapter 6, Gerard Hughes, explains how the tax system is used to encourage saving in occupational and personal pension plans. Current estimates of the cost of tax expenditure on private pensions are presented and it is shown how the cost has grown over the last two decades. Comparisons are made between the cost of tax expenditure on private pensions and the cost of direct expenditure on contributory old age pensions and on the means-tested non-contributory old age pension. The picture that emerges will be, to some people, a rather startling one: the State spends almost as much on tax reliefs for private pensions as it spends directly on the contributory and non-contributory public pension schemes put together, and, on current trends, it will soon be spending more on the private than on the public schemes.

This in turn raises basic questions of equity. Gerard Hughes shows that the coverage of private pension plans is very uneven with poor coverage for low skilled workers and good coverage for highly skilled workers. He argues that the interaction of generous pension subsidies and good coverage for high income workers results in an inequitable outcome with most of the benefits of tax relief for private pension saving going to those at the top of the income ladder. He suggests some policy options that would introduce more equity into the tax arrangements for private pensions: -

• Granting pension tax relief as a tax credit so that it has the same value for all taxpayers;
• Phasing out the tax-free lump sum so that all benefits are payable as a pension;
• Establishing a relationship between the income cap on pension contributions and gross average earnings that would focus the tax reliefs on middle and lower income groups; and
• Introducing an annual tax on the returns on pension investments.

In considering such options in relation to the Irish pension system, it is useful to consider the experience of other countries. Our institutional arrangements and our dependence on funded pensions make our pension system closer to the UK than to any other EU country. The UK pension system has undergone many changes in recent years, but has also had considerable problems – pension misselling, deficits in company pension schemes, and the subsequent closure of defined benefit schemes (where pension payments are linked to final salary) to new members, and problems with key institutional components of private sector pension provision such as Equitable Life. In Chapter 7, Sue Ward gives a critical analysis of the pension system and pension policy in the UK.

The next section summarises our views on a realistic

future for pension provision that would be both equitable and efficient.

1.3 A REALISTIC STRATEGY FOR FUTURE PENSION PROVISION

Chapter 3 shows that there is considerable uncertainty associated with population forecasts. Uncertainty associated with population forecasts creates considerable policy dilemmas. Policy proposals such as those in the National Pension Policy Initiative (Pensions Board, 1998) assume populations projections are certain. The Report states (p. 66) : 'The central projection shows that the elderly dependency ratio will decline slightly between 1991 and 2006 and then rise rapidly'. It also cites a projection undertaken by Irish Pension Trust in 1997 that the dependency ratio will more than double between 2006 and 2056. The Department of Finance (1998) also relies extensively on these later projections, as does the Minister for Finance (Dail Speech / December 14, 1999) in announcing the National Pension Reserve Fund. The pensions industry has been even more certain in its assumption of population change. The problem is that policies are argued for and introduced to meet a problem whose overall scale and cost is uncertain. Future planning for uncertain outcomes requires flexibility and the development of policy options.

However, only one option is emphasised. The Pensions Board and the pensions industry argued for increased funding as a solution to projected population change. But increased funding as a solution has considerable implications for the economy wide allocation of resources as pension contributions constitute a substantial part of national saving. It also necessarily results in a pensions industry heavily dependent on professionals (accountants, lawyers, actuaries fund managers) and hence is expensive. It is arguable as to whether funding is, in fact, a solution to a future increase in those aged 65+, because a pensions system (whether funded or pay-as-you-go) is designed to deliver future output to those in retirement. This transfer cannot be guaranteed by any pension system.

Private sector pension provision via funding is very dependent on tax reliefs. This is especially evident in the case of individual pension plans such as PRSAs, as tax reliefs are emphasised in all marketing material.

What should be the basis for realistic pension provision? The following four elements could form the basis for an efficient and equitable pension system: -

1. One element could be a universal State pension, based on citizenship. Such a basic pension would not be means tested. It would be comprehensive, cost effective and address in particular the issue of those who have atypical working careers (part-time, periods out of work, frequent changes in employer), poor coverage amongst females, those in certain occupations (building and catering), and those who are not in the labour force. What about the cost? Chapter 6 argues that the State already spends substantial sums on existing private sector pension provision via tax reliefs. The value of these tax reliefs approximates the value of State based pension payments. It is doubtful that these tax reliefs are a cost effective way of delivering pension income, and instead could usefully be curtailed to fund a future basic pension.

2. A second element would be a second State pension based on Social Insurance contributions which would top up the universal pension.

3. A third element would be provided by private sector schemes, but private sector pension arrangements

need to be more cost effective and less driven by tax planning.

4. A fourth element is a change in working/retirement patterns.

Ensuring a viable pension system funded by the State by taxation of employers and employees is not necessarily dependent on increasing the working age beyond 65. But one way to help ensure the solvency of pension systems is to ensure that the retirement age is 65. Too many employers have used a firm's pension to fund early retirement packages, to the subsequent detriment of existing employees. This issue has already been addressed to some extent for public sector employees. For some employees, working beyond 65 is an option, and such an option should be extended as widely as possible on a voluntary basis, with subsequent increases in tax revenues and the ability to fund pensions. Even if pension payments were actuarially neutral (i.e. a longer working life was compensated by higher pension payments), increasing the possible working age would help finance pension payments because the dependency ratio would be reduced.

Finally, what should be the role of the National Pension Reserve Fund? Funded pensions do not introduce any greater certainty into pension payments. As argued in Chapter 4, the National Pension Reserve Fund is unlikely to earn the projected rates of return initially expected. Diversifying such a large proportion of national savings outside Ireland makes it more difficult to fund projects that would increase future productivity and the ability to pay for future pensions. A Pension Reserve Fund is inequitable in the sense that the current generation of retired persons have lower pensions than they might otherwise obtain in order to fund pensions of a future generation. This fund should be directed to purchase Irish Government debt only,

with the eventual aim of cancelling this debt and abolishing the Fund.

To date, discussion of population change and a projected growing number of those aged 65+ has been dominated by future pension provision. The cost of future pension provision is one aspect. But population change also has considerable implications for social care, for policies for those living alone and for health/nursing home care. These are issues that will eventually affect all retired persons and hence, pension and other policies also need to be considered in an integrated way.

As we approach the centenary of the introduction of old age pensions in Ireland, what better way would there be to mark it than by having in place a fair, equitable and efficient pension system that renews the promise of a dignified old age for Irish citizens in the 21st century?

Notes

1. For example, a Report for Forfas (1998) expresses concern about the reducing level of investment by Irish pension funds in the domestic economy (Forfas, p. 207) and suggests increased funding for infrastructure. Following a request from the Minister for Finance, Irish pension funds are reported to have agreed to increase the proportion invested in venture capital (p. 211).

References

Forfas (1996), *Shaping our Future, A Strategy for Enterprise in Ireland in the 21st Century*, Dublin: Forfas.

Pensions Board (1998), *National Pensions Funds Policy Initiative*, Dublin: Pensions Board.

Chapter 2

Incomes of Retired Persons in Ireland

BY JIM STEWART

2.1. INCOMES OF RETIRED PERSONS

A useful starting point in considering issues and risk in relation to pension provision is to examine how effective the current pension is in delivering pension income to retired persons. There is, however, very limited data on the current sources and level of income of retired persons in Ireland. One of the sources is the Household Budget Survey, produced by the Central Statistics Office (CSO). We used this data source to examine the current distribution of retirement incomes by age and by gender. The Household Budget Survey also has some data on the current investment income and assets of the retired population, for example housing ownership, which we also consider.

Data Description

The data relates to income and expenditure of a random sample of 7705, 7877 and 7644 households over a 12-month period during 1987, 1994–95 and 1999–2000, respectively. The data is published in the form of average weekly incomes or expenditure broken down into various categories (Central Statistics Office, 1997, appendix 4), and is made available to researchers. Of particular interest for this study are the income and sources of income of single retired persons. These were selected from the entire sample and resulted in a study group of 723, 992 and 827 persons for the three survey periods respectively. This data was further examined by gender and by age. The data thus consists of three randomly chosen cross-section samples at different points in time. This means that, for example, rising income levels through time may not mean that incomes have necessarily increased for participants in earlier surveys, as different households may be included in different surveys. Nevertheless, given the relatively large sample size and the fact that households are included on a random basis, it allows us to make inferences about likely income levels and sources of income for the entire population.

The accuracy of the data depends on the accuracy of information given by independent households. Certain expenditures are likely to be understated and it is also possible that sources of non-pension income may be understated.

Previous research has shown: -

1. Occupational pensions provide a small proportion of income to retired persons.

From Household Budget Survey data (Connell and Stewart, 2004), it can be shown that in Ireland the State old age pension is the main source of income to households headed by a person aged 65 or over. This is true whether sources of income are examined or the absolute number of households in receipt of a State old age pension compared with an occupational pension is considered. For example for the survey years 1999-2000 those households headed by a person aged 75+ obtained an average of just over 20 per cent of their household income from an occupational pension, compared with 48 per cent for State pensions. Using a different data source (The ESRI Living in Ireland

Survey), Gerard Hughes reports in Chapter 6, Table 6.6, that for the year 2000, 56 per cent of income came from social welfare pensions for those aged 65+. Our results exclude the income from benefit in kind such as free electricity, etc. Such a result is surprising. There is a long established, well funded occupational pension system in Ireland with coverage of around 50 per cent of the employed work force. In 1999, Irish pension funds had the third highest proportion of investment in equities (after the US and UK) and equity markets performed particularly well in the period 1980-1999. Hence, Irish pension funds in the period 1980-1999 experienced some of their highest historic returns ever recorded.

2. Replacement rates are low (Pension Income as a Proportion of Income at work).

Using data from Household Budget Surveys does not allow us to estimate replacement rates (proportion of income replaced by pension payments) as we are not tracking the same individual from work to retirement. As noted above, the State old age pension provides the main source of pension income to retired persons and as the basic contributory pension is 27 per cent of average industrial earnings for males and 40 per cent for females (January 2004) it is safe to assume that pension incomes of retired persons are well below pre-retirement incomes. For the survey year 1999-2000, total pension income of households with HOH (Head of Household) aged 65-74 amounted to 48 per cent of the average industrial wage (using the average industrial wage for 1999) and for those households where the HOH was aged 75+ pension income amounted to 44 per cent of the average industrial wage. The average industrial wage is a very imperfect measure of retirement income, as employee income may increase with age and the average industrial wage for females is approximately two-thirds that of males.

3. The older you are the lower your income.

For all survey periods examined, income of retired persons declines with age. This may be partly explained by rising wage levels while pension payments are fixed at retirement or are indexed to prices.

A report by the Council of the European Union (2003) shows relative measures of poverty among those aged 65+ for the EU (15) using data from the European Community Household Panel for 1999 (ECHP). The report states (p. 25) "that poverty risks vary considerably from one country to another and that they are usually higher for women than men" and that "the oldest pensioners (aged 75 and over) tend to be more at risk of poverty than younger pensioners". Differences in income levels between men and women for those aged 65+ are largely due to lower levels of occupational pensions by women (Council of the European Union, 2003, p. 87).

Of particular interest is that for one measure of relative poverty (proportion of persons with incomes less than 60 per cent of median disposable incomes for those aged 65+ compared with those aged 0-64), Ireland had the highest poverty measure amongst EU countries at 34 per cent (Council of the European Union, 2003, Chart 14 and Table 2). A lower definition of poverty (50 per cent of the median) reduces the ranking by poverty of those aged 65+ in Ireland to third position. It is also of interest to note that there appears to be a trend towards increasing poverty (measured by income of retired persons as less than 60 per cent of median income). Data for 2001 for Ireland shows that 42 per cent of persons aged 65+ had incomes below 60 per cent of median employment income (Pensions Commission, 2004, p. 69). Not surprisingly, public pension expenditure as a per cent of GDP is the lowest in Ireland compared with other EU countries (Pensions Commission, 2004, p. 61), although this may be partly explained by differences in old age dependency and variations in the level of payments in kind.

The data cited so far for Ireland relies on household incomes which are adjusted to take account of household size and composition. This is necessarily an arbitrary procedure. From data in the Household Budget Survey we identified single person households in order to focus in particular on retirement incomes of single people and on possible differences between male and female retirement incomes. This data source confirms that:-

4. Female retired persons have lower incomes than male retired persons.

5. Sources of retirement income are different comparing males and females. Females are more dependent on State old age payments.

The next section examines these issues in greater detail.

2.2 SOURCES OF RETIREMENT INCOME

Table 2.1 shows the proportion of households headed by a female for the entire survey for the three survey years. The data shows a clear trend through time towards an increasing proportion of households headed by a female for all age cohorts, except for those aged 55-64 and 65-74.

Table 2.1 Female per cent of HOH by Age Cohort

Age	1987	1994/1995	1999/2000
15-24	46.5	60.5	65.4
25-34	13.8	26.5	32.4
35-44	10.4	16.6	23.0
45-54	13.5	17.7	21.5
55-64	26.2	21.8	24.0
65-74	36.3	37.4	34.1
75+	42.8	47.3	48.1

For Richer, For Poorer

Of particular interest is that the proportion of households aged 75+ with a female HOH increases from 42.8 per cent in the 1987 survey to 48.1 per cent in the 1999-2000 survey.

Other statistical evidence also shows a rise in the number of single person households. Table (2.2) shows those living alone in 2002 and projected numbers in 2021. For comparative purposes Table (2.2) also shows the total population of those aged 65+ and projected population for the year 2021. Table (2.2) shows that while those living alone are a minority of the population aged 65+ they are projected to increase from 26 per cent to 30 per cent of those aged 65+ by the year 2021. Approximately two-thirds of elderly living alone were female in 2002 and this is projected to fall slighly to 65 per cent by 2021. The next chapter examines in greater detail how changes in certain parameters, for example longevity, may affect these projections.

Table 2.2 Elderly Living Alone in 2002 and Projected in 2021

		2002	2021
Males living alone	Aged 65-69	10845	21979
	Aged 70+	27169	52196
Females living alone	Aged 65-69	14570	26847
	Aged 70+	61242	109700
Total		113826	210722
Total population females	Aged 65+	246846	375836
Total population males	Aged 65+	189155	322651
Total male and female		436001	698487

Source: Connell and Pringle (2004), Population Ageing in Ireland, report prepared for the National Council on Ageing and Older People, Tables (3) and (6).

Table 2.3 shows the proportion of single female households as a percentage of the total number of single households in the Household Budget Survey data. Table 2.3 mirrors Table 2.1 in a number of respects. A majority of single person households are found in the age group 15-24, this ratio falls and then rises so that the greatest proportion of female single person households is found in the oldest age categories. Table 2.3 also shows that for each survey period single females account for over two-thirds of single person households in the oldest age category 75+.

Table 2.3 Single Female Living Alone by Age Cohort and As a Per Cent of Age Category

Age	1987	1994/1995	1999/2000
15-24	55.2	63.0	55.6
25-34	33.3	42.9	34.2
35-44	45.2	42.2	40.6
45-54	39.9	37.1	47.6
55-64	52.8	42.2	59.4
65-74	66.1	60.4	61.0
75+	67.1	66.0	67.5

Source: Household Budget Surveys

Table 2.4 shows gross weekly income of those living alone by age cohort. The averages shown in this table are slightly reduced because a small number of individuals' incomes were capped (Connell and Stewart, 2004, p. 147) in order to preserve confidentiality. Column (1) shows average incomes. Because of the variation in incomes reflected in the average, it is also useful to consider median incomes (the most frequently occurring amount) shown in column (2). The main features of Table 2.4 are the substantial drop in income for both single males and females comparing the cohort immediately preceding retirement and subsequent retirement. This gap increases for each survey period. The Table also shows a lower income for all years for each age cohort over 65 for females compared with males. This is true whether average or median incomes are compared.

Lower pension income for females compared with males may be explained by atypical working careers for women (this is well documented for the UK by Ginn, 2003). Increased longevity for women coupled with partial or no indexation of pension payments also results in a declining proportion of occupational pension income. If pension payments were to become actuarially fair, assuming pension contributions remain the same, income inequalities would be exacerbated.

Table 2.4 Gross Weekly Income (€) of Those Living Alone by Age Cohort

	1987				1994/1995				1999/2000			
	M		F		M		F		M		F	
Age	(1)	(2)	(1)	(2)	(1)	(2)	(1)	(2)	(1)	(2)	(1)	(2)
55-64	143	81	121	65	188	109	190	109	349	167	274	163
65-74	103	77	89	72	141	102	128	95	194	129	172	124
75+	117	79	90	74	150	78	122	96	208	139	159	125

Note: Column (1) shows average incomes and column (2) median incomes.

Tables 2.5 and 2.6 give greater detail on relative sources of income to retired persons. Table 2.5 shows average sources of pension income for single males for each survey period and by age cohort. Table 2.6 shows the same information for single females. Average incomes are used rather than median income because the median income for some sources is zero. A comparison of Tables 2.5 and 2.6 shows that for all survey years and age cohorts single females are more dependent on pension income than single males. Both tables also show that dependence on pension income (State plus occupational) generally increases with age.

Table 2.5 Sources of Pension Income of Single Males - Average Amounts Per Week in Euros

Age	N[1]	Total gross mean household income	Total pension income from all sources	Mean income from state employ. pension	Mean income from other employ. pension	Mean income from state old age pension[2]	Mean income from other welfare pensions[3]
Year 1987							
55–64	151	143.69	21.44	6.83	2.98	0.00	11.07
65–74	295	102.60	72.58	11.59	9.79	49.61	1.57
75+	186	116.84	80.74	19.31	9.13	50.75	1.54
Year 1994/95							
55–64	155	187.34	40.58	10.45	16.72	0.00	13.41
65–74	218	136.71	97.88	6.50	19.64	67.96	3.78
75+	150	145.73	107.70	15.83	16.78	72.60	2.46
Year 1999/2000							
55–64	102	348.64	48.45	12.79	19.39	0.00	16.27
65–74	170	194.12	129.43	22.56	24.51	75.00	7.35
75+	127	208.28	161.87	48.02	23.99	84.71	5.15

Notes:
1. Number of respondents
2. Old-age contributory and non-contributory pensions and retirement pensions for those aged 65–67.
3. Widows' and orphans' contributory and non-contributory pensions, invalidity pension and disablement pension.

Table 2.6 Sources of Pension Income of Single Females - Average Amounts Per Week in Euros

Age	N[1]	Total gross mean household income	Total pension income from all sources	Mean income from state employ. pension	Mean income from other employ. pension	Mean income from state old age pension[2]	Mean income from other welfare pensions[3]
Year 1987							
55–64	135	117.64	46.43	3.57	7.96	0.00	34.89
65–74	151	86.95	72.98	10.58	8.70	29.94	21.48
75+	91	87.48	76.55	11.96	7.90	41.61	15.07
Year 1994/95							
55–64	113	185.22	87.97	27.02	18.02	0.00	42.93
65–74	333	124.27	107.86	15.69	15.92	42.89	33.36
75+	291	119.36	103.08	9.26	18.51	52.43	22.88
Year 1999/2000							
55–64	149	274.39	71.78	24.85	10.34	0.00	36.58
65–74	266	172.05	134.58	21.87	24.97	60.16	27.59
75+	264	158.95	133.54	17.02	22.80	65.13	28.58

Notes:
1. Number of respondents
2. Old-age contributory and non-contributory pensions and retirement pensions for those aged 65–67.
3. Widows' and orphans' contributory and non-contributory pensions, invalidity pension and disablement pension.

A comparison of Tables 2.5 and 2.6 also shows that for all survey years and for each age cohort (with the exception of single males aged 64-75 for the survey period 1994-1995), single females are more dependent on state sources of pension income (State old age pension plus other welfare pensions). In contrast to single males, the relative dependence on State old age and other pensions for single women increases if those aged 65-74 are compared with those aged 75 plus. An indication of the relative differences in income levels between males and females can also be seen in the numbers in receipt of a means tested pension (non-contributory State old age pension and widows pension). For all survey years examined for both age cohorts (with the exception of 1987/88 for those aged 65-74), a higher percentage of females were entitled to means tested welfare payments.

Table 2.7: Sources of Income to Retired Persons Living Alone for 1999-2000 (Per Cent)

	Pension Income/ Total Income	State Employ. Pension/ Total	Other Emply. Pension/ Total	State Welfare/ Total
Males aged 65-74	66.7	11.6	12.6	42.4
Males aged 75+	77.7	23.0	11.5	43.1
Females aged 65-74	78.0	12.7	14.5	51.0
Females aged 75+	84.0	10.7	14.3	59.0

Table 2.7 summarises sources of pension income from various sources for the survey year 1999-2000. Some indication of replacement rates can be found if income from pensions for both single males and females from Tables 2.5 and 2.6 is compared with the average industrial wage. For females average pension incomes are approximately 33 per cent of the average industrial wage for 1999, 31 per cent for

males aged 65-74 and 40 per cent for males aged 75+. Higher ratios are obtained for single females if pension incomes are compared with female average industrial wages, and lower ratios for single males if pension incomes are compared with male average industrial earnings.

It is well known that average incomes may be distorted by a small number of high incomes. Using the median income may not be very useful as a substantial number of those included in the survey report zero income from particular sources, and hence the median income from a particular source such as occupational pension may be zero.

Table 2.8 Number of Individuals Living Alone Reporting Income from Different Pension Sources for Persons Aged 65+

	1987		1994-1995		1999-2000	
	Male	Female	Male	Female	Male	Female
Income from pension and/or Social Security	212	448	332	597	264	504
State employment pension	28	55	36	58	44	52
Other employment pension	36	64	73	80	59	98
State Social Security[1]	189	403	306	549	237	466
State Social Security only[2]	149	335	224	462	162	358
Occupational pension only[3]	23	45	26	48	27	38

Notes:
1. Refers to all income from Social Security
2. Individuals receiving other sources of pension income were excluded
3. Individuals receiving any Social Security payments were excluded.

Table 2.8 shows the number of those aged 65+ who reported any income from occupational or State pensions.

This data confirms our earlier conclusions. State social security payments were the main sources of retirement income. For the survey period 1999-2000, 90 per cent of males and 92 per cent of females reported pension income from this source. Secondly, females are more dependent on State social security payments than males. For the same survey period 61 per cent of males compared with 71 per cent of females reported State social security payments as their only source of pension income. Comparing the three survey periods, there has been a small decline in the proportion of males reporting State social security as their only source of retirement income.

Sources of Investment Income and Gender

Some studies have found that sources of investment income for retired persons vary with gender. However, an examination of reported investment and property income from this data shows that average incomes from these sources are low, irrespective of gender. The largest single income source was reported as 'other investment income', with 20-40 per cent of persons reporting income within this category for the survey years 1987 and 1994-1995, with reduced numbers for 1999-2000. Females were slightly less likely to report income in this category for the earlier years, although the amounts in all cases were small. Over 90 per cent of respondents reported no income from property or stocks and shares. Again, in common with households with two or more persons, most single elderly retired persons live in an owner occupied house. The trend through time has been for the proportion living in owner occupied housing to rise and those living in local authority rented accommodation to fall. So that for the survey year 1999/2000, 80 per cent of single person households owned their own house. This is slightly lower than for all households where the head of household is aged 65+, in the Household Budget Survey, where the proportion is 84 per cent. There was also little difference between house ownership by single persons by gender or on the basis of those in receipt of a non-contributory old age pension (which is means tested) compared with a contributory old age pension (which is not means tested). This is likely to be because own home ownership is excluded from assets considered as 'means' in assessing eligibility for the State old age non-contributory pension (Source:- http://www.welfare.ie/).

2.3 CONCLUSION

The evidence presented in this chapter shows that social welfare pensions constitute the main form of income to single persons aged 65 and over. This chapter also reported the majority of single person household are female, that their retirement income is lower than that of single person male households or households with two or more persons. They are more dependent on social security retirement income, have fewer sources of other income such as stocks and shares, and hence lower accumulations of wealth in comparison with other households types.

If retirement income patterns are generally as reported in the HBS data, then increased longevity will mean a fall in retirement income, which will be particularly acute for single females. With longer female life expectancy, a greater prevalence of 'actuarially fair' life pension payments will further compound these issues. It is difficult to see current pension policies which emphasise complex financial products with considerable tax relief as incentives, providing a major source of future retirement income. The growth of defined contribution retirement income (where pension benefits are a function of returns on an accumu- lated fund) coupled with increased longevity will also mean that pensions incomes on retirement will fall in real terms.

Hence, it is likely that State sources of old age pension income will remain as important if not become more important in pension incomes of retired females. The next chapter considers issues of demographic change in greater detail.

Notes

1. For example a Report for Forfas (1998) expresses concern about the reducing level of investment by Irish pension funds in the domestic economy (Forfas, p. 207), suggests increased funding for infrastructure and, following a request from the Minister for Finance, Irish pension funds are reported to have agreed to increase the proportion invested in venture capital (p. 211).

References

Central Statistics Office (2004), Quarterly National Household Survey Pensions Update, Quarter 1 2004, September 2004, Dublin: Central Statistics Office, available at www.cso.ie.

Central Statistics Office (1997), Household Budget Survey 1994-95, Dublin: Stationery Office, pn 3934.

Connell, P. and J. Stewart (2004), "Income of Retired Person in Ireland: Some Evidence from Household Budget Surveys", in G. Hughes and J. Stewart (eds.) Reforming Pensions in Europe: Evolution of Pension Financing and Sources of Retirement Income, Cheltenham: Edward Elgar.

Connell, P. and D. Pringle, (2004), Population Ageing in Ireland, Report prepared for the National Council on Ageing and Older People.

Council of the European Union (2003), Draft Joint Report by the Commission and the Council on adequate and sustainable pensions, 6527/1/03, Brussels: Council of the European Union, available at http://europa.eu.int/comm/employment.

Forfas (1996), *Shaping our Future, A Strategy for Enterprise in Ireland in the 21st Century*, Dublin: Forfas.

Ginn, J. (2003), *Gender, Pensions and the Lifecourse*, Bristol: The Policy Press.

Pensions Board (1998), *National Pensions Funds Policy Initiative*, Pensions Board.

Pensions Commission (2004), *Pensions: Challenges and Choices The First Report of the Pensions Commission*, London: Stationery Office, available at *http://www.pensionscommission.org.uk/*.

Chapter 3

Demographic Projections: Defusing the Time Bomb

BY PETER CONNELL

3.1 INTRODUCTION

Population forecasts are the single most important factor in discussions about future pension policy. The stated arguments for changes to the US social security retirement system by the second Bush administration, which involve increasing private saving but reduced social security spending, are based on demographic change (see report of White House press conference, New York Times, February 3, 2005). This is also the general argument of the influential World Bank Report, *Averting the Old Age Crisis* (1994)). The general assumption is that the number of those aged 65+ will grow dramatically and that the ratio of those at work to retired persons will be much larger than today. This, in turn, will require a considerable increase in the transfer of resources, for example State old age pensions, to those in retirement. However, this chapter argues that for Ireland, while it is highly likely that there will be an increase in the numbers aged 65+ in the next 20 years, there is more uncertainty in the forecast dependency ratios (the ratio of those at work to those not at work). These ratios are likely to remain lower in Ireland than in other countries. However, forecasts beyond 20 years are subject to greater uncertainty in relation to both the increase in the number of those aged 65+ and associated dependency ratios.

Projections of the future cost of State social security pensions are largely determined by population projections, given that there is a minimum socially acceptable level of retirement income. Projections of future growth in the numbers aged 65+ also have implications for the cost of future private sector pension provision. The previous chapter reported evidence in relation to a growing projected population of those aged 65+ and that approximately two-thirds of these are expected to be females. What is often not made clear in discussions of population projections is the inherent level of uncertainty involved in these projections.

Table 3.1 Population Projections – a Hazardous Enterprise

	Projected population	
	2001	2006
	(000s)	(000s)
National Pensions Board (1993)	3481	3424
Fahy and Connell (1995)	3622	3654
CSO (1995)	3649	3720
DKM (1995)	3621	3762
Connell and Stewart (1999)	3792	3960
CSO (2001)	3836	4053
Actual (2002)	3917	
Likely (2006)		4172

Table 3.1 shows that successive attempts to project population have consistently underestimated population growth. For example, projections by the National Pensions Board

compiled in 1993 for the year 2006 were already an underestimate of approximately 20 per cent by 2001. In the Irish
context, the level of migration has proved to be the great
imponderable in population projections. Because of the
relative absence of migration by those aged 40 +, it has
proved possible to generate reasonably accurate forecasts of
the numbers aged 65 and over for up to 25 years into the
future. However, the old age dependency ratio and the
relative proportion of GDP required to support the older
population cannot be forecast with anything like the same
degree of accuracy.

3.2 REASONS FOR THE VARIABILITY IN POPULATION PROJECTIONS

Migration

A key variable that has proved very difficult to forecast is the
level of migration. The variable historic pattern of Irish
migration is illustrated in Fig. 3.1. Population projections
produced in the 1990s assumed either zero net migration or
even out-migration whereas Fig. 3.1 shows large and
growing in-migration from the mid-1990s onwards. Even
more recent projections have failed to anticipate the
continued scale of in-migration following the slowdown in
economic growth after 2000. In the last two years, net
migration has continued at a level of over 30,000 per
annum. Recent population projections published by the
CSO use two different assumptions regarding the scale of
in-migration to Ireland in the period 2002-2036. These are
referred to in the projections as 'high' and 'moderate'
migration assumptions and, cumulatively, they result in
populations in 2036 that differ by over 500,000. If these
projections were extended by a further 20 years up to 2056
the resulting populations would differ by about 750,000.

Fig. 3.1 Patterns of Migration

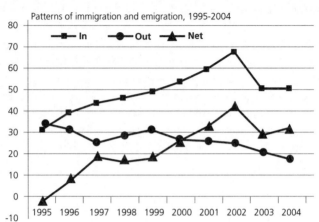

Life Expectancy

While underestimating net migration has been the main reason for the failure to project population accurately, changes in life expectancy have been a contributory factor.

Table 3.2 Improved Life Expectancy

| Life expectancy at specified ages | | | | | | |
Males	0	40	50	60	70	80	90
1980-82	70.1	32.6	23.6	15.9	9.7	5.4	2.9
1985-87	71.0	33.1	24.0	16.0	9.7	5.3	2.8
1990-92	72.3	34.4	25.2	16.9	10.4	5.7	3.0
1995-97	73.0	35.1	25.8	17.5	10.6	5.8	3.0
2001-03	75.0	37.0	27.8	19.2	11.9	6.5	3.3
Females	0	40	50	60	70	80	90
1980-82	75.6	37.3	28.0	19.5	12.2	6.7	3.5
1985-87	76.7	38.0	28.7	20.0	12.6	6.8	3.3
1990-92	77.9	39.2	29.8	21.1	13.5	7.3	3.6
1995-97	78.5	39.8	30.3	21.5	13.7	7.5	3.7
2001-03	80.3	41.4	31.9	22.9	14.8	8.2	4.1

Table 3.2 shows actual improvements in life expectancy at various ages, from age zero to 90, over the past two decades. For example, life expectancy for a female aged 60 years has increased from 19.5 years in 1980-1982 to 22.9 in 2001-2003. Variations in improvements in life expectancy from period to period have proved an added complication in accurate forecasting. For example, between 1991 and 1996 life expectancy for males aged 70 improved by a very disappointing 0.2 years while in the period 1996-2002 there was a very substantial increase of 1.3 years.

Table 3.3 shows some international comparisons of life expectancy. The table shows that, by international comparisons, there is significant scope for further improvements in Irish life expectancy. For example, for males aged 65 in Ireland life expectancy is 15.4 years compared with 16.9 years for Sweden.

Table 3.3 Life Expectancy – International Comparisons

Life expectancy at specified age					
Males	0	45	65	75	85
Belgium	75.1	32.3	15.8	9.3	4.7
Ireland	75.1	32.3	15.4	8.9	4.6
Austria	75.8	32.9	16.3	9.8	5.0
Finland	74.9	32.1	15.8	9.3	4.8
Sweden	77.7	34.3	16.9	9.9	4.9
Females	0	45	65	75	85
Belgium	81.1	37.4	19.7	11.8	5.7
Ireland	80.3	36.6	18.7	11.2	5.8
Austria	81.7	37.8	19.7	11.8	5.8
Finland	81.5	37.0	19.0	11.1	5.2
Sweden	82.1	38.1	20.0	12.2	6.1

Source: Council of Europe, 2003.

3.3 POPULATION FORECASTS

Assumptions

The accuracy of any population projections reflects the assumptions made about births, deaths and migration. The most widely recognised measure of fertility is the 'total period fertility rate' (TPFR). This is defined as the average number of children born to a cohort of women who experienced, throughout their childbearing years, the fertility rates of the calendar year in question. Irish fertility rates have declined significantly over the past four decades, reaching their lowest point in the mid-nineties. Since then the TPFR has recovered to 1.98. The assumption adopted for the current projections is outlined in Table 3.4. This sees a gradual decline in the fertility rate up to 2021 and remaining constant thereafter. The recent CSO population projections adopt three different assumptions regarding fertility. The assumption described in Table 3.4 is a hybrid of the 'medium' and 'low' assumptions used by the CSO. In the medium term this would still see Ireland experience among the highest fertility rates in Europe. The average TPFR for northern European countries is currently only 1.7.

Table 3.4 Fertility Rate Assumption

	2002	2006	2011	2016	2021-56
TPFR	1.98	1.95	1.85	1.80	1.75

Life expectancy assumptions are as shown in Table 3.5. Changes in life expectancy for those aged under 40 have been very slight over the past 20 years so the main focus in these assumptions is on the older age groups. As Table 3.2 shows, there were considerable gains in life expectancy for both men and women in these older age groups in the period since 1986. Men aged 60 gained 3.2 years and women gained 2.9 years. It is assumed that this trend will continue up to 2036. This would see life expectancy for males aged 60 increase from 19.2 in 2001 to 26 in 2036, with a corresponding increase for females from 22.9 to 29.0.

Table 3.5 Life Expectancy Assumptions

- Improvements in survivorship for those over 40 years of age
- 1986-2002 trend extrapolated to 2036
- Constant thereafter
- Male life expectancy at 60 to rise from 19.2 years in 2001 to 26 years in 2036
- Female life expectancy at 60 to rise from 22.9 years in 2001 to 29 years in 2036
- Trends consistent with gains in life expectancy in European countries

Because variation in migration is such a key variable in Irish population forecasts we use two different migration assumptions as shown in Table 3.6. For comparison purposes, this table also shows the 'high' migration assumption used by the CSO in their latest projections. The key difference between assumption M1 and assumption M2 is the long-term forecast regarding the scale of in-migration. While it is reasonable to assume that a fairly high level of net in-migration will take place over the next 20-25 years, it is extremely difficult to predict population flows in and out of the country beyond that time.

Table 3.6 Migration Assumptions

	M1 assumption	
	2002-11	+30,000 per annum
	2011-21	+20,000 per annum
	2021-56	+10,000 per annum

- **M2 assumption**

2002-11	+30,000 per annum
2011-21	+15,000 per annum
2021-31	+10,000 per annum
2031-56	+ 0 per annum

- **CSO M1 assumption**

2002-16	+30,000 per annum
2016-26	+20,000 per annum
2026-36	+15,000 per annum

Detailed Population Projections

Table 3.7 and figure 3.2 shows how sensitive population projections are to different assumptions regarding net migration. Table 3.7 shows that by the year 2036, forecast population based on the CSO high migration assumption is 400,000 higher than the M2 low migration assumption used in the current projections. If the CSO assumption is projected forward to 2056 it generates a population 750,000 higher than that based on our M2 assumption. Without significant net in-migration, the Irish population will stabilise at some point in the next 40 to 50 years. Predicting when this will happen involves predicting when the scale of net in-migration falls back from its current high level of 30,000 per annum. Under migration assumption M1 this will not happen under after 2046 while under the lower M2 assumption it is likely to occur 20 years earlier.

Table 3.7 Population Projections

Year	Connell M1	Connell M2	CSO M1
2006	4173	4173	4166
2036	5371	5185	5669
2056	5519	5143	

Fig. 3.2 Projected Population 2002-2056

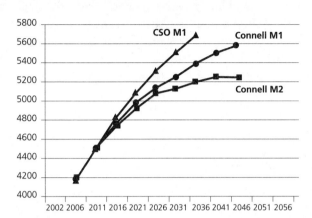

Dependency Ratios

Figure 3.3 shows that in the long-term the forecast old age dependency ratio (i.e. the numbers aged 65 and over divided by those aged 15 to 64) almost trebles by 2051 from 0.16 to 0.44. However, it also shows that in the medium term, that is by 2026, it will only have increased to a figure of 0.24 which is close to the current average of most western European countries. Measured in these terms, and in a timescale where we can have at least some degree of confidence about the accuracy of the forecasts, it appears that Irish policy makers have a 20-year window to address issues around old age dependency before we are confronted with scenarios currently being dealt with by our neighbours. By 2051 it is projected that this measure of old age dependency will converge for most west European countries at about 0.45.

Note that the forecast old age dependency ratio in the long-term reflects a growing number of those aged 65 and over and a decline in the number of those aged 15 to 64. This later decline is mostly explained by the lower assumed net migration (10,000 per annum from 2021 onwards) compared with 30,000 currently. Historically migration in and out of Ireland has been strongly influenced by economic conditions. It may be unrealistic to assume that economic conditions in Ireland will consistently result in net inward migration in the very long-term. On the other hand recent experience has shown that net migration has been consistently underestimated and it may be that our assumptions also underestimate future in-migration.

Fig. 3.3 Changes in Old Age Dependency Ratios for Ireland and Selected European Countries

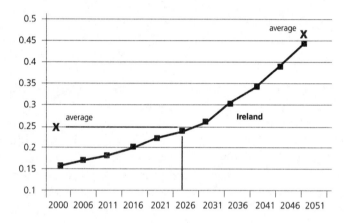

Ireland is not the only country where the level of immigration can create considerable uncertainty in relation to future population and dependency ratios. For example the Pensions Commission (2004, p. 9) for the UK states that an assumption of net inward migration of 300,000 per annum reduces the forecast dependency ratio from 47.3 per cent to 42.1 per cent. Mitchell and Pain (2003) estimate that gross inward migration into the UK has doubled over the last 20 years to 370,000 for the year 2000. They forecast these trends to continue in the future.

3.4 LABOUR FORCE FORECASTS

The issue of the sustainability of future pension payments is partially a function of dependency ratios. More accurately, it is a function of the size of economic wealth of society in the future, in particular incomes per capita. The ratio of those aged 65 and over to the projected labour force is often used as a surrogate for economic dependency and the ability to provide for future pension payments. At this point, it is worth noting that the recently published population and labour force projections produced by the CSO include population projections for the period up to 2036 but labour force projections only up to 2016. The report states that the rationale for restricting the labour force projections to this relatively short time span is 'because of the uncertainty involved in projecting labour force participation rates in the longer term'[1]. The size and shape of the future labour force is a function of the underlying population but also of assumptions regarding the likelihood that different groups in the population will be economically active. This obviously adds another layer of uncertainty on top of those associated with projecting future populations.

Table 3.8 shows the assumptions made in our labour force projections up to 2026.

Table 3.8 Labour Force Assumptions

- Largely follows assumptions made by Blackwell & Assoc. for National Spatial Strategy updated by 2004 data
- Male participation rates to stay largely constant
- A slight increase in participation rates for those aged 65 and over
- Female rates

- for those aged 35 to 64 higher than Blackwell anticipated
- these rates projected to continue rising
- high participation rates of those now aged 25 to 34 to feed through to much higher rates for those aged 45 to 54 after 2016
- cohort 55 to 59 participation rate 2004: 42 per cent 2026: 0. 8 per cent

Under the M1 migration assumption, and applying the participation rate assumptions described in Table 3.8, the labour force is projected to increase from 1.92 million in 2004 to 2.52 million in 2026. The annual rate of increase will slow from 2.4 per cent currently to about 0.6 per cent by the early 2020s. Even this rate of growth will be highly dependent on continuing high levels of migration into the country. Almost two-thirds of the additional 600,000 in the labour force by 2026 will be related to in-migration with the remaining one-third reflecting changes in labour force participation rates. Increased female participation rates will add 160,000 to the labour force, with smaller changes in male participation rates adding 40,000.

Table 3.9 Labour Force Projections, 2006-2026

	Male	Female	Total	Change	Per cent change per annum
2004	1120	801	1921		
2006	1160	854	2014	93	2.4
2011	1247	958	2205	191	1.9
2016	1302	1030	2332	127	1.2
2021	1352	1090	2442	110	0.9
2026	1388	1130	2518	76	0.6

The labour force in 2026 will be considerably older than at present. In 2001, 32 per cent of the labour force was aged 30 or under; by 2026, this will fall to about 24 per cent. On the other hand, 30 per cent of the labour force is currently aged 45 or older. By 2026, this will have risen to close to 40 per cent.

The projected ageing of the workforce could have implications for future pension provision. However, one view from the European Commission states: -

> There is no consensus regarding the effect of ageing on productivity and technical progress. One view is that an ageing labour force would be less dynamic and, therefore, less productive. An alternative view is that the increased scarcity of labour would create incentives to seek improvement in the utilization of factors, so accelerating the rate of technical progress. The latter implicitly takes an endogenous view of the growth process, that is that the rate of technical progress can be influenced by economic choices. A related idea is that ageing might induce a shift in investment from physical to human capital, with a potentially positive effect on productivity (Pench 2000).

Finally, Table 3.9 shows a measure of dependency based on labour force projections as distinct from population projections. This ratio, usually referred to as the old age economic dependency ratio, is calculated by dividing the size of the labour force by the numbers aged 65 and over. Currently there are over four people in the labour force for each person aged 65 or over. This is projected to decrease to about three people by 2026. However, both the current situation and the projected ratio for 2026 is much more positive than the EU average. Eurostat data published in 2000 indicated that the economic dependency ratio for the 15 member states at that time was less than 3.0 and projected to fall to close to 2.0 by 2025[2]. This suggests that Ireland will continue to have a distinct 'competitive advantage' over many EU countries in terms of the sustainability of State social security pensions for at least another 20 years.

Table 3.9 Old Age Economic Dependency, 2004-2026

	Labour Force	65 and over	Ratio
2004	1921	436	4.4
2006	2014	478	4.2
2011	2205	538	4.1
2016	2332	620	3.8
2021	2442	712	3.4
2026	2518	804	3.1

3.5 CONCLUSION

The published Life Table for Ireland for 2000-2002 shows significant improvements in life expectancy occurred during the 1990s, mostly concentrated in the older age groups. Continuing improvements in life expectancy, combined with rising numbers currently in the age cohorts 45 to 64, mean that the numbers aged 65 and over will increase by 85 per cent by 2026. Projecting the number of older people beyond that date is dependent on assumptions about migration about which there can be little certainty 20 year hence. Inward migration in recent years has continued at higher than anticipated levels. Future levels of migration are difficult to predict and are likely to be tied to economic growth.

Levels of in-migration will have a strong influence on future population projections and dependency ratios. A key variable, which affects the ability to pay future pension increases, is the future wealth of society. Future output and income is in turn partly a function of the size of the labour force. We argue that continued high in-migration and increased female participation rates, particularly in age cohorts over 45, will boost the size of the labour force. However, the main factor in determining changes in the size of the labour force is projected in-migration. Based on our higher assumptions about in-migration, the labour force is projected to increase by 600,000 by 2026.

On the basis of these forecasts, our overall conclusion is that Ireland's dependency ratios remain low by international standards for the next 20 years but increase thereafter. In particular, the ratio of those in the labour force to those aged 65 and over will fall only gradually in this period and will be high by international standards in 2026. Hence, the issue of the cost of medium pension payments is not as important for Ireland as for some other countries. Forecasts after this period are characterised by uncertainty. This means that pension policy decisions being made currently must necessarily be flexible and adaptable to a wide range of future possible outcomes. For example, current policy emphasises channelling a large proportion of national savings into pension funds and pension type products and in addition compulsory pension savings have been discussed. Such policies, which may be based on inaccurate forecasts of future dependency ratios, could reduce current and future growth rates and the ability to fund future pension payments. The next chapter critically examines the proposed solutions to higher future pensions costs via increased use of private sector pension provision.

Notes

1. Central Statistics Office, *Population and Labour Force Projections, 2006-2036* (Dublin, 2004).
2. See Population Division, UN Secretariat, Expert Group Meeting on Policy Responses to Population Ageing and Population Decline, 2000 at http://www.un.org/esa/population/publications/popdecline/fotakis.pdf

References

Blackwell, Jonathan and Associates (2001) *Population, Labour force And Housing Demand Projections*, Final Report to National Spatial Strategy.

Central Statistics Office (1995) Population and Labour Force Projections 1996-2016, Pn 1455, Dublin: Central Statistics Office.

Central Statistics Office (2001), Population and Migration Estimates 2001, Dublin: Central Statistics Office.

Central Statistics Office (2003) Population and Migration Estimates, April 2003 (With Revisions to April 2002), Dublin: Central Statistics Office.

Central Statistics Office (2004), Population and Labour Force Projections, 2006-2036, Dublin: Central Statistics Office.

Connell P. and D. Pringle (2004), *Population Ageing in Ireland*, Report prepared for the National Council on Ageing and Older People, Dublin: National Council on Ageing and Older People.

Connell, P. and J. Stewart (1999), Demographic Projections and Population Ageing in Ireland, in G. Hughes and J. Stewart (eds.), *The Role of the State in Pension Provision: Employer, Regulator, Provider*, Dordrecht: Kluwer Academic Publishers.

Council of Europe, (2003), *Recent Demographic Developments in Europe*, Strasbourg: Council of Europe.

Fahy, T. and P. Connell (1995), *Health and Social Care Implications of Population Ageing in Ireland, 1991-2011*, Dublin: National Council for the Elderly, Report, no. 42.

Fahey, T. (2001), 'Trends in Irish fertility rates in comparative perspective', *The Economic and Social Review*, 32(2) July.

Mitchell, J. and N. Pain (2003), "The Determinants of International Migration into the UK: A Panel Based Modelling Approach", London: National Institute of Economic and Social Research.

National Pensions Board (1993), *Developing the National Pension Board*, Dublin: Stationery Office.

Pench, L. (2000), Ageing and Economic Growth in Europe, CSIS Conference on Graying of Industrial World, 25-26 January 2000.

Pensions Commission (2004), *Pensions: Challenges and Choices The First Report of the Pensions Commission*, London Stationery Office, available at www.pensionscommission.org.uk.

UN Secretariat (2000), Expert Group Meeting on Policy Responses to Population Ageing and Population Decline, 2000, Population Division, UN Secretariat, available at http://www.un.org/esa/population.

World Bank (1994), *Averting the Old Age Crisis*, Oxford: Oxford University Press.

Chapter 4

Private Sector Pensions: Funding, Risks and Costs

BY JIM STEWART

A viable pension system requires a solvent (and hence profitable) private sector pension system. Around 52 per cent of the work force in Ireland are members of an occupational or personal pension scheme (CSO, 2004). For the year 2003, 26 per cent of those in employment were members of either a defined contribution type scheme (where pension payments are strictly a function of the size of the pension fund) or of defined benefit schemes, which are subject to a minimum funding standard and are monitored by the Pensions Board. These schemes in turn are dependent on the solvency and ability of financial institutions in the private sector to manage pension schemes and pension fund investments, and ultimately pay retirement income. Dependence on these institutional arrangements will increase as current pension policy emphasises both collective and individual saving, and the accumulation of assets from which pension income will be paid. Some examples are the National Pension Reserve Fund, and individual retirement schemes such as Personal Retirement Savings Accounts (PRSAs).

4.1 THE EFFECT OF FALLING STOCK MARKETS AND RETURNS

There are serious issues relating to the efficiency and viability of the current funded pension system. The period 1980-1999 was a period of large stock market gains. Irish pension funds in 1999 had the third highest proportion of funds invested in equities yet survey data for 1999 shows that occupational pensions provided only a small part of pensioners incomes. Future returns on equities, and pensions derived from them, are likely to be lower than in the period 1980-1999. Pension funds with high equity exposure suffered particularly in the recent stock market downturn (2000-2002), and have not fully recovered their asset values. In addition, recent academic research has shown that commonly used assumptions about the long run historic returns from equities and hence, extrapolations of these returns, have been too high. Dimson, Staunton and Marsh (2002) estimate that for Ireland the historic extra return to equities compared with government debt is just 3 per cent per annum. The Pension Commission for the UK (2004, appendix C p. 80) suggests a real portfolio return of 4.54 per cent (gross of all costs). Average costs per annum are estimated to be just over 1 per cent, reducing the real return to 3.5 per cent, but costs for small schemes could be as high as 2 per cent per annum reducing real returns further to 2.5 per cent per annum. These estimates compare with an assumed real return of 5 per cent in a report by the Pensions Board (1998, p. 14). Inflation as measured by changes in the consumer price index over the five years to 2003 was 3.5 per cent (Source: CSO www.cso.ie/principalstats). Hence, in nominal terms the return assumed by the Pensions Board amounts to 8.5 per cent per annum. These calculations do not make any adjustments for uncertainty discussed later in this chapter or the effects of the tax deductibility of pension fund contributions and the exemption from tax of pension fund income, as discussed in Chapter 5.

A decline in capital values and projected income means that current pension schemes have estimated liabilities greater than the current market value of assets. Recently, the Pension Board in Ireland has stated that between 40 and 50 per cent of all defined benefit schemes (where pension payments are a function of final salary and not investment returns) have estimated liabilities greater than assets (Pensions Board, 2004, p. 5). These estimates are based on particular assumptions which may or may not turn out to be correct, but assuming they are accurate it means that these pension schemes, will not be able to pay pensions as guaranteed in employment contracts.

This position is not unique to Ireland. As of July 2004, the aggregate pension scheme deficit for FTSE companies using a generally accepted accounting standard (FRS17) amounted to £42 billion. For the year 2003, estimated liabilities for FTSE companies were higher at £55 billion but for the same year the estimated full cost of securing equivalent benefits with an insurance company has been estimated at £125 billion (Source: Lane et al, 2003 p. 3, & 13). Similar issues also affect pension funds in the Netherlands and Switzerland (L'Observatoire des Retraites, 2004, p. 29). Partly as a result, some commentators consider that "companies are inherently unsuitable institutions for providing pensions", (Martin Wolf, *Financial Times*, August 20, 2004).

Falling stock market values are not the only reason for the crisis in private sector pension fund provision. The Pensions Commission (p. 94) in the UK describes the crisis as " the end of a fool's paradise", of lack of recognition of increased longevity and low contributions to pension funds disguised by abnormal stock market gains. The crisis has also been exacerbated by lower returns on Government debt.

One effect of pension deficits and low returns has been a closure of defined benefit (DB) schemes to new members and increased use of defined contribution (DC) type schemes. So that for the UK, one survey found that 38 per cent of large schemes (1000+ employees) were closed to new members, 62 per cent of medium schemes (100-999 employees) and 45 per cent of small schemes (less than 100 employees) (Source: Occupational Pension Scheme Regulatory Survey, 2003, p. 12). The Pensions Commission (2004, p. 84) forecast that in future years defined benefit type schemes will only exist in the public sector in the UK. This is also likely to be the case in Ireland where there is also evidence of a move away from DB type schemes to DC schemes. For the year 2003, the number of DB schemes fell by 11 per cent, although there was some small growth in membership (Source: Pensions Board Annual Report 2003, p. 20). The report goes on to comment that "within the private sector, membership of defined benefit schemes remains less than that of defined contribution schemes" (Pensions Board Annual Report, 2003, p. 22).

4.2. THE GROWTH OF FUNDING

In recent years, it has been generally argued that funded pensions were the solution to the problem of pension provision. However, in a number of cases, funded pension schemes have become part of the problem in future pension provision. Pension systems in all countries have been subject to considerable criticism. In particular, pay-as-you-go systems have been criticised because it is argued they represent future unsustainable liabilities. The *Financial Times* (September 28, 2003) comments: -

> France, Germany, Italy and Spain are the European countries facing the most severe challenges to the sustainability of their pension systems.

A growing proportion of elderly, it is argued, will make pay-as-you-go (PAYG) pension systems unviable. The solution, it is claimed, is a much greater emphasis on funding future pensions. To facilitate this, there has been a switch in emphasis from compulsory/institutional arrangements to volun-tary/individual pension arrangements. Some examples:-

1. An increased emphasis on individual pension provision. In the UK, the 'green paper' on pensions states (p. 118), "The government will *continue to encourage individual saving*". Ireland has seen the introduction of a new personal pension product (PRSA), championed by the main pensions regulator in Ireland, the Pensions Board. The US government also proposes to reduce the value of social security pension payments and increase pension income from individual savings accounts (New York Times, January 10, 2005). This proposed change has aroused considerable opposition (see, for example wwwaarp.org/social_security/).

2. Increased use of pension arrangements referred to as Additional Voluntary Contributions (AVCs). Typically, these are used where employees are not entitled to a full occupational pension because, for example, pension scheme rules require 40 years of employment, but the maximum possible employment is less than this. The amounts contributed are voluntary, benefit from increasingly generous tax treatment, and are invested and managed totally within the private sector.

3. In Canada (http://www.cppib.ca) and Ireland (http://www.ntma.ie), the introduction of a national pension fund, and in Norway, a National Petroleum Fund (http://www.norges-bank.no). In all cases the intention is that the fund will partly fund social welfare pensions.

    The main thrust of these changes has been to

increase the dependence of some of the currently retired and future retirees on funded schemes, and on individual provision.

Implicit in the general debate on funding are issues revolving around the attempt to secure resources now that will be needed by retired persons in some years time. However, the difficulty is that whatever type of pension system is used, the attempt to secure now, a future claim on real goods and services is subject to uncertainty and variables that cannot be controlled. Blake (1995, p. 251) for example states: –

> No generation can store for its own retirement the consumer goods that it itself produced. Each generation is wholly dependent on the next generation, not only for the types of goods that it consumes in retirement, but also for the quantity of goods that it is able to consume, since the next generation also chooses the prices of these goods.

Blake further argues that it is impossible for the current generation to pre-commit the next generation to provide a particular stream of consumption goods. For this reason, Blake considers that "all pension schemes whether funded or not are in reality pay-as-you-go schemes" – a point which has been accepted by the EU Commission in a report on procedures to increase coordination of pension systems within the EU, referred to as the "open method of coordination of pensions" (EU, 2003, p. 43). The report states "all pension schemes, regardless of the financing mechanism they use (funding or pay-as-you-go), transfer a share of the current output of the economy from the active to the retired". The UK Pensions Commission (2004, p. 12) further argues "that it is a delusion to believe that funding pensions magically reduces the challenge of an ageing society".

In view of the contrast between the above quotations and those who argue for the benefits of pre-funding, it is worth exploring some of the possible different effects of a PAYG and a funded pension system.

The first point is that the method used to pursue a future transfer of real resources to retired persons may affect future growth and output, and the ability to secure a future claim. For example, the effectiveness with which current transfers to a fund are invested will affect economic growth. The decision to fund may also affect economic growth, through effects on domestic savings. Davis (1995, p. 160) considers that funding would increase saving, as does the World Bank (1994, p. 173), although the World Bank (1994, p. 307) also notes that the impact of pension financing on savings has been a source of "considerable controversy on both theoretical and empirical grounds".

Hughes (1996), in an extensive survey of the literature, finds no conclusive evidence that funding increases savings or that PAYG pension systems reduce savings. Advocates of funding social welfare payments, such as the National Academy of Social Insurance in the US, consider that funding of social security pensions "can increase national savings and thereby national income". Some argue that while funding may not increase the overall level of saving, it changes the composition of saving from short term assets such as bank deposits to long-term assets such as those traded on capital markets (Davis 1995, p. 162). Hence, even if savings rates do not increase, the flow of funds into long-term capital and investment may do so. Some suggest, for example that the capital stock may be higher with a funded pension scheme (Miles, 1977, p. 172).

The World Bank report argues that funded occupational schemes have earned much higher returns than publicly managed pension funds and reserves (1994, p. 174). However, the evidence for this statement is limited to a study by Davis (1993) of pension fund performance in nine industrial countries and appendix A.12 of the World Bank Report that shows the portfolio distribution of pension fund assets in eight OECD countries in 1970 and 1990. The World Bank Report further states (p. 175) that "to the degree that occupational pension funds have increased long-term saving or directed savings towards productive investment, they have enhanced growth in their countries and in the broader economy".

There are also considerable costs associated with managing an investment fund (discussed later in this chapter). There may also be adverse effects resulting from pension funds choice of assets (buying shares of large firms which are more liquid) and hence a bias against small firms. Concentration of share ownership and management of portfolios by pension funds can result in growth in trading volumes in securities and an emphasis on short run investment decisions. There may also be effects on corporate governance that may not always be positive (Myners Report, 2001; Stewart, 1996). Because of possible adverse effects on corporate governance, some contended that the establishment of a National Pension Reserve Fund in Ireland, which owned large blocks of Irish equities, would necessarily result in poor corporate governance and investment decision making (Davis, G. 1999).

The pensions industry, governments, and the European Commission, have argued that funding will reduce future pension costs by increasing current savings and by investing those savings to earn high real rates of return. For example, in Ireland the National Pensions Policy Initiative in recommending the establishment of a national pension reserve fund states (p. 110) "by having a genuinely invested fund" actual costs of future pensions would be reduced, and as noted earlier, a real return of 5 per cent is suggested (National Pensions Policy Initiative p. 14). It is also argued that by improving the flow of funds for investment, economic growth will be increased.

However, large stock market losses over 2000-2002 and increased risk associated with institutional provision have drawn attention to difficulties with funded pension systems. Controversy relating to the establishment of a National Pension Fund in Ireland has increased following Stock market falls (2000-2002) and subsequent falls in the value of the National Pension Reserve Fund. Falls in the value of the fund were limited because of delays in passing necessary legislation and the consequent inability to invest in assets other than cash. From April to December 2001, the fund earned a return of 3.3 per cent, −16.1 per cent in the year 2002, despite holding average cash balances in excess of 26 per cent of the total portfolio (National Pensions Fund Annual Report, 2002, p. 27), and 12.8 per cent in 2003. Strangely, the Annual Report (2002, p. 23) comments that since its launch in April 2001, the National Pension Reserve Fund (NPRF) has performed relatively well, given market conditions, compared with the average Irish managed fund and the Fund's own long-term strategic benchmark. A Canadian Fund established for similar purposes reported similar falls during this period.

4.3 THE ROLE OF INSURANCE COMPANIES IN PENSION PROVISION

Life Insurance companies are a key part of private sector pension provision. There has been extensive recent coverage of financial problems associated with life assurance companies such as Equitable Life and Britannic Group. One result of financial problems in the life insurance industry is that returns on pension products and other long-term savings contracts have been reduced substantially. Projected annual bonuses have not been paid. A recent report argues that financial products (referred to as 'with profits' policies), whose returns depend on paying bonuses that are a function of investment returns, are in 'terminal decline' (*Financial Times*, August 20, 2003). Ultimately this means that the size of pension that can be bought is also reduced.

Many pension schemes invest their funds and provide benefits through some form of insurance contract. At a minimum, certain contingencies (e.g. death or disability of members) are insured by a pension scheme. The standard type of investment structure used is either a unit–linked insurance contract or a with-profit contract. In a unit-linked arrangement, the scheme buys units in one of the investment funds of the insurance company, for example the Irish Equity fund, a fixed interest fund or perhaps a managed fund incorporating a broad mix of assets. The value of the scheme's units fluctuates with the value of the underlying fund. The assets in the underlying fund remain the property of the insurance company, the scheme's assets are the units it holds in the fund. A with-profit contract may guarantee a benefit at retirement equivalent to a specified rate of return, or this may be merely a projected or expected return. Where investment performance exceeds the rate guaranteed, the insurance company may declare an additional bonus, assuming assets invested earn above this minimum rate.

Larger pension schemes may manage their own funds. Typically, the scheme would place its funds with one or more fund manager having agreed in advance aspects of investment strategies, key performance indicators and fee structure. But even these schemes may use life insurance companies as fund managers, and invest via managed funds.

Individual schemes such as Additional Voluntary Contribution schemes (AVC schemes) and the recently introduced Personal Retirement Savings Accounts (PRSAs) are also often managed by firms in the financial sector such as Life Insurance companies.

4.4 WHAT ARE THE RISKS?

A greater reliance on managed pension funds for future pension payments necessarily involves risk and uncertainty. Due to their long-term nature (up to 40 years of contributions and 20 years or more of benefits), pension contracts are subject to considerable risk and uncertainty. Who bears the risk and the extent of that risk in a pension fund system is partly a function of whether it is a defined benefit scheme or a defined contribution scheme. It is also a function of the institutional structure to collect pension contributions and arrange eventual pension payments to pensioners, but these institutional risks are insufficiently recognised. One possible reason for this is that economists (especially financial economists) assume risk profiles match individuals risk preferences. Bodie and Merton (1998, p. 217) comment:

> Risk aversion is a characteristic of an individual's preferences in risk-taking situations. It is a measure of willingness to pay to reduce one's exposure to risk. In evaluating trade-offs between the costs and benefits of reducing risk, risk-averse people prefer the lower risk alternatives for the same cost.

An assumption that investment preferences matches risk preferences ignores the institutional context in which pension products are provided

Institutional Risk

These risks can be broadly divided into three areas: − (1) risk arising through inappropriately priced contracts, for example guaranteeing rates of return that are too high (based on historic patterns) or selling annuity type products on the basis of underestimates of longevity; (2) inappropriate investment policies; and (3) risk arising through bad management. All three sorts of risk are difficult for regulators to judge accurately. They may be impossible for outsiders to judge.

For many pension contracts risk can arise from a number of different sources and not just investment policy. For example, pension contracts that involve indirect investment via an insurance company or fund manager(s) or indeed where the member's pension is funded by the purchase of an annuity, can give rise to third party risks. For instance, the outcome of a contract taken out with an insurance company may be wholly or partly dependent on the continued existence of that company (albeit in perhaps a different legal form). It is difficult for those entering contracts with an insurance company to know the nature of other contracts which may (in distress situations) take precedence in the distribution of investment returns (as in the Equitable Life Case), or whether contracts are written based on assumptions about longevity which are false (as in the Britannic Insurance case, source: The Guardian, January 7, 2003). In general, insurance companies are also exposed to uncertainty where the statistical distribution of outcomes is not known.

Pension fund trustees may consider direct investment using a selected fund manager or a number of fund managers rather than a more 'hands on' approach which gives them greater involvement and control, and hence counter-party risks remain. Consider the situation where the primary fund manager invests scheme monies in a fund operated by yet another third party fund manager (for example, an Irish fund manager might invest in Far East equities via a Far East equity fund operated by an overseas fund manager). The pension scheme now has, in addition to the counter–party risk associated with the primary fund manager, the risk associated with this additional third party (Stewart and McNally, 2003).

Perhaps the greatest risk that pension scheme trustees have to contend with is likely to arise from the quality of management in both the primary insurance/fund management providers and the various sub-providers. It is very difficult to judge the nature of these risks but they nonetheless exist.

Risk in Defined Benefit versus Defined Contribution Schemes

There is increased risk to pension scheme members from membership of a defined contribution type scheme (including personal pensions) compared with membership of a defined benefit type scheme. In a defined contribution plan, contributions are specified. Future benefits depend on future net rates of return, the duration of working and retirement periods, and annuity prices on reaching retirement age. This investment, disability and longevity risk is borne by the employee. In defined benefit plans, the pension formula is determined in advance although it may depend on years of employment and salary over a certain period (e.g. last three years of employment). In effect, the employer undertakes to pay members a pension related in some manner to career earnings. The member may or may not be required to contribute to the scheme depending on the scheme rules and provisions. The employer commits to cover any shortfall in funding. The principal risk to a member of a defined benefit scheme is that the sponsor-company may not pay pensions as envisioned in employment contracts. This could arise through fraud, as in the Maxwell case, or more likely through corporate failure, as in the Enron case. Effectively these sorts of risks arise because the employer does not contribute sufficient funds to an externally managed fund. Other risks can arise where the sponsoring employer, though profitable and solvent, changes the terms and conditions of the pension scheme, for example a switch from a defined benefit to a defined contribution scheme, or where an employer closes down. In one recent case in the UK, an employer announced that they would shut down in order to avoid funding a pension fund deficit (Maersk in the UK – part of an international shipping group) although this decision was subsequently reversed after regulatory and other intervention (Source: *Financial Times*, January 1, 2003). There are also risks if pensions are provided via an annuity, since the stream of pension payments (annuity payments) is dependent on the financial health of the annuity provider. It has been generally supposed that such payments streams were without risk, but to help ensure its survival, Equitable Life decided to cut payments to pensioners (annuitants).

Investment Risk

Investment risk is now widely recognised. The high returns of the period 1970 to 1999/00 are seen as an aberration. Dimson, Marsh and Staunton (2000, p. 224) conclude that "future returns from equities are likely to be lower than those achieved in recent decades". The return from equities is not likely to be much greater than the return from bonds in future years (Dimson, Marsh and Staunton, p. 4). An important reason for this is that while equities may have higher returns they also have higher risk. One well-known expert on pension funding, Bodie comments that governments and bureaucrats "fall into the trap of thinking that shares are not risky in the long-term" (*Financial Times*, July 26, 2003). In particular, he argues that because of risk equity shares are particularly inappropriate for those on low incomes or with job insecurity. The issue can be summarised as investment versus insurance. We may invest (or be advised to invest) with a particular risk distribution, but we insure (or are advised to insure) with quite a different risk distribution. We avoid events that would be catastrophic (our house burning down) even though there is a low probability of this occurring (Davies, 2000, p. 117).

The stock market recession (2000-02), coupled with

lower investment returns slowing economic growth, has also reduced the ability of employers to continue to fund defined benefit type plans. In order to reduce risk, many employers have switched to defined contribution plans for new entrants, where pension payments are a function of fund returns and are not a function of final salary or contribution years. Hence, volatility in stock markets and the value of pension funds means volatility in pension payments. Concialdi and Lechvalier (2003, p. 275) comment that this "shows pension fund schemes to be the outcome of a kind of lottery in which some generations emerge as winners and others as losers".

Risk from Uncertain Values of Tax Reliefs

Returns to pension products are partly a function of the value of tax relief. Tax reliefs can be claimed by the individual and the employer, and the accumulating fund is tax free. Only the eventual payment is taxed, although lump sums are tax-free. If future flows of individual income are uncertain so is the value of tax relief. Financial products whose returns are partly / wholly a function of tax relief are most attractive to those with high marginal tax rates and with a high probability of future flows of taxable income.

4.5 COSTS

A key issue in assessing the efficiency of funded pensions is their cost (in terms of investment costs, administration etc.). Low projected returns to pension funds (by historic standards) coupled with the existing cost structure will mean that net returns to invested funds are low, capital accumulation with the same level of saving is reduced, and funds available for distribution as pensions will be lower than in the past, with implications for pension income. Hence, for a given level of income, the required stock of savings is higher.

Even though returns have on average been negative over the period 2000-2002, costs of managing all pension schemes were positive, as they are partly determined by funds under management not fund performance. For example, within Ireland many pension schemes have reported falls in asset values in this period but administration costs have increased (excluding the costs of trading). The relationship between increasing costs but declining assets under management can be found for example for the ESB and An Post pension schemes for the year 2001, and for the Telecom Eireann pension scheme for the year ending March 2002. For the ESB pension scheme, fund assets declined from €2,912 million in 2001 to €2,702 million in 2002, but disclosed charges (excluding costs of trading assets) increased from €1.6 million to €3.07 million. It is important to note that disclosed costs are not the same as total costs. The Pensions Commission in the UK estimates that administrative charges calculated in terms of annual reduction in yield (RIY) vary from 0.2 per cent to 0.5 per cent for occupational schemes, with charges up to 1.5 per cent for small company schemes, but average 0.8 per cent for personal pensions (Pensions Commission, 2004, p. 80). To these costs must be added implicit costs that vary as function of turnover within the fund and markets where funds are invested (US markets are cheaper than those in the UK or Ireland because of the absence of stamp duty). This means that an estimated real gross portfolio return of 4.54 per cent reduces to 4.08 per cent after implicit costs and falls further to 3.5 per cent after explicit costs (Pensions Commission, 2004, p. 80). Implicit costs may also be higher than those estimated by the Pensions Commission because of the effects of a main fund manager passing the funds to sub-managers for investment. These sub-managers may, in turn, have implicit costs not reflected in management charges.

Costs become much more important with low

For Richer, For Poorer

projected returns in the future. Estimates for the UK are that average costs will amount to 20 per cent of gross returns. Costs are a function of the size of the fund so that small funds and personal pensions are likely to be 2-3 times as expensive as large funds (Pensions Commission, 2004, p. 78 and 80). In Ireland, pension schemes are smaller than in the UK and hence average costs are likely to be higher. In private sector schemes in the UK for the year 2000, 46.9 per cent of members were in schemes with 10,000 or more employees and 75.5 per cent of members were in schemes with 1,000 or more employees (Government Actuaries Department, 2003, Table 3.1). For comparative purposes, this data was compared with membership of defined contribution schemes and those defined benefit schemes that are monitored by the Pensions Board in Ireland in relation to their solvency. These schemes are mostly but not totally in the private sector. There were no schemes with more than 10,000 members and just 20 per cent of members were in schemes with 1,000+ members (Source: Pensions Board Annual Report, 2001, pp. 23-24).

For personal pensions (PRSAs), management charges are capped at 5 per cent of funds contributed and a further 1 per cent of funds managed (Pensions Board, 2003, p. 5). These maximum charges have also generally become the minimum charges. Pension management charges are likely to be much higher for individual schemes such as AVC schemes. Total charges for Public Sector AVC schemes were estimated to vary from 12 to 20 per cent of the overall value of the fund. These estimates exclude an annual management charge of 0.75 per cent (Commission on Public Sector Pensions, 2000, p. 351). The extensive range of costs and charges that may be levied on pension and life insurance savings products in Ireland are described by the Irish Financial Services Regulatory Authority (2005) but their overall cost is not estimated.

In contrast the cost of running the State old age pension

system is substantially lower. For the UK costs of the State pension system have been estimated at 0.1 per cent of the value of the pension liability compared with 0.2 per cent for large occupational schemes and 1 per cent for personal pensions (Pensions Commission, 2004, p. 251). Costs may also be expressed as a per cent of contributions. On this measure Hughes and Whelan (1996) report that the costs of administering funded schemes in Ireland amounted to 5 per cent of contributions for 1994. This compares with 1.5 to 2 per cent of contributions for State old age pensions (Hughes and Whelan, 1996b, p. 110). For the US and the UK, the cost of administering State old age pensions is reported to be even lower at 1 per cent of contributions, while costs of various private sector schemes vary from 2 per cent to 8 per cent.

4.6 WHAT ARE THE SOLUTIONS?

The Savings Gap

The fall in stock market values in 2000-2002 which reduced capital values, with associated lower expected future returns and lower annuity rates, means that for the same level of pension income a much larger sum needs to be accumulated than in periods prior to the year 2000. Hence, there is considerable interest in what level of savings is now required for a given replacement rate. This issue is particularly acute for those depending on personal pension plans and those in strictly actuarially based pension plans (where pension payments are a function of the accumulated lump sum). One estimate is that a current annual salary of €25,800 (the average industrial wage) and a target replacement rate of two thirds would require 13 per cent of salary saved for 40 years (Society of Actuaries, 2003). However, this sum would account for just over half the target pension level, with the balance made up of the State old age pension. Higher salary levels require a far greater level of pension contribution. Such calculations are based on strong assumptions, for example a 6 per cent real rate of return and that existing favourable tax regimes for pension provision remain.

Average contribution rates from both employer and employee to defined contribution schemes have been reported at just 10 per cent of salary (Irish Association of Pension Funds, Pension Benefits Survey, 2002). The same survey reported employer contributions to DC plans at 5.9 per cent and another survey reported employer contributions at 6.6 per cent of pay (Kehoe, 2003, p. 11). Such low contribution rates have prompted a comment that "the real pensions time bomb in Ireland is the inadequacy of contribution rates to Defined Contribution plans" (Kehoe, 2003, p. 11). The difference between projected contribution rates and current contribution rates has been referred to as the Savings Gap. This gap has been quantified by Life Strategies (2004) as an average savings shortfall of €3,300 per person in the labour force. This report notes that estimates of the 'savings gap' are very sensitive to the assumptions made, for example assumed rates of return, and replacement income was estimated on the basis of what is 'required' rather than as a fixed per cent of salary. But it is important to note that the 'savings gap' as estimated is also very sensitive to the assumed level of the State old age pension.

The 'savings gap' is not unique to Ireland. A recent estimate for the UK is that 60 per cent of the working population aged over 35 are not currently saving enough for retirement. Thirty-two per cent are not making any savings provision (Pensions Commission, 2004, p. 160). Those with poor or no pension provision are concentrated amongst those working part-time, self-employed and women (Pensions Commission, 2004, p. 160).

Similar issues of poor pension coverage exist in Ireland. PRSAs were specifically aimed at such groups (atypical employees without existing occupational pension coverage) but response has been slow. Since the inception of the scheme in February 2003 to November 2004, 37,000 individuals signed up. This compares with 1.170 million individuals who opened a Special Savings Investment Account (SSIA) between May 2000 and April 2001 when the scheme closed. The 37,000 who opened a PRSA account may also not all represent an increase in pension coverage as there may be substitution from other sorts of pension coverage. Assuming they all represent 'new' pension coverage, they account for approximately 8 per cent of those in employment without pension coverage in 2004 (Source CSO: 2004a, and 2004b, Table 2 and 11). In addition, we should note that average amounts contributed are unlikely to provide for adequate replacement pensions. For the first year in which PRSAs were available, the average annual individual contribution amounted to approximately €2,500 (Pensions Board press release August 6, 2004). Using Society of Actuaries estimates, this would be insufficient to create a post retirement income of 50 per cent including the State old age pension. One reason for the relative lack of take up compared with SSIAs has been the absence of matching employer contributions. Undoubtedly PRSAs are also more complex than SSIAs (Niall Doyle, 2004). Another issue is that while costs are certain returns are risky, not only from variable investment returns, but risk that can arise from the value of tax reliefs associated with pension products. A major component of the return to PRSAs (emphasised in advertising) is the value of personal tax relief and the value of tax relief is most uncertain for those with atypical working patterns (part-time working, seasonal work) interspersed with periods out of work – the very target group that PRSAs are aimed at.

Other proposals have suggested turning savings products (particularly SSIAs) into pension type products using tax incentives. If applied to all holders of SSIAs, this would be expensive in terms of tax forgone and inequitable in the sense that those with higher incomes (largest SSIA accounts) are likely to benefit the most. Furthermore, the majority of beneficiaries are likely to be those who are already members of occupational pension schemes rather than the target group – that is, those without current pension provision. Another proposal is to introduce a new pension product (the Pensions Savings Investment Account) which would be modelled on the SSIA and involve the State making matching contributions (Life Strategies, 2004). A possibility of allowing fixed interest deposit type invest-ments would also reduce risks and costs. This would also reduce risk from variations in the value of tax relief but to provide incentives at the same rate as SSIAs would be costly. There would also be an issue of targeting those without current pension coverage.

One suggested way of reducing costs under a modified PRSA scheme is to place a cap on contributions so that the benefit from a modified PRSA could not exceed the prevailing rate of State welfare pension (Kehoe, 2003, p. 19), and the combined benefit (State old age pension plus modified PRSA) could not exceed 60 per cent of the average industrial wage (Kehoe, 2003, p. 19). Such proposals are in effect a contributions related social welfare pension, with the added complication that sums are routed through a PRSA provider, and then to the National Pension Reserve Fund (Kehoe, 2003, p. 8). Undoubtedly, reducing risk and increasing returns would make PRSAs more attractive, but also more costly and may still not achieve target coverage rates.

Sometimes it is argued that poor pension coverage is a result of the fact that "many people are imprudent, short-sighted or reluctant" to provide for pensions (Pensions Board, 1998, p. 9). Another argument is that there may be considerable ignorance about financial products, hence the proposal by the Insurance Federation to introduce a module on insurance products organised by the Irish

Insurance Federation into the school curriculum. More generally, financial regulators attempt to reduce information asymmetries and increase consumer awareness. IFSRA states one of its aims is to provide "independent information on financial products in plain English" (see http://www.ifsra.ie/). The Financial Services Authority in the UK states "We aim to help consumers become better informed about financial matters" (see http://www. fsa.gov.uk/).

An assumption that lack of information is the main barrier to pension provision assumes that those without pension provision have the financial resources to enter into long-term contracts and that their current expenditure patterns are in some sense 'irrational'. To illustrate this latter point consider the proposal from the Irish Insurance Federation that pension accounts be opened for children in which the State would pay €10 and sponsors €50 a month with tax relief until the age 18 – a proposal that has been enthusiastically welcomed by SIPTU (press statement, 30 May 2004; *Irish Times*, 11 September 2004). Such a proposal would provide a very limited solution to low pension coverage because of the likely small sums involved. It is likely to have considerable adverse distribution effects (children from wealthy backgrounds would benefit to the greatest extent) and be poorly targeted (those who are likely to be members of a pension scheme will benefit to the same extent as those who are not). The main determinant of the level of pension is lifetime salary. This in turn is a function of qualifications achieved and life skills, for example knowing a foreign language – all of which involves spending resources during school years. The other main determinant of the level of pension is staying healthy. However, the infrastructure and organisation of health supporting activities for school children, which has a considerable influence on lifetime health, is expensive and requires considerable current expenditure.

Increase the Retirement Age

Proposals to increase savings and/or reduce pension costs are often discussed in association with proposals to increase the retirement age. In Ireland for example, changes in legislation will require new entrants to the public service to retire at 65 rather than 60 (Public Service Superannuation [Miscellaneous Provisions] Act 2004), as recommended by the Commission on Public Sector Pensions (par. 15.15.17). There are also proposals to prevent compulsory retirement at age 65 in order to comply with the EU directive on equal treatment, which has been welcomed by bodies representing older people such as Age Concern in the UK (The Guardian, June 22, 2004). Issues raised by extending the working age if voluntary and cost neutral, so that deferred pensions are actuarially enhanced, are unlikely to be controversial. In the UK, it is possible to choose to defer the State old pension in return for higher future payments (Department of Work and Pensions, 2002, pp. 101-102). Available evidence appears to show that increasing longevity is not associated with increasing disability (Pensions Commission, 2004. p. 30). Hence, it is likely that many of those aged over 65 are not prevented on health grounds from extending their working lives. In addition, those in certain occupations may welcome an opportunity to extend their working lives and future pension payments, but others in less desirable occupations would not voluntarily choose to extend their working lives. Such effects could exacerbate income inequalities in old age. These effects would be further compounded by those who have left the workforce on disability benefits.

What is more controversial is whether it should be made compulsory to work beyond 65. Such a proposal has been rejected by trade unions (*Irish Times*, September 11, 2004). In effect, extending the working age involves a reduction in pension benefits, unless there are additional pension benefits. One possible effect would be to cause some of those who would have retired at 65 to leave the work force and seek disability benefit.

As discussed in the next section, regulation is a key aspect of private sector pension provision and proposals to reform current pension systems have also included proposals for regulatory reform.

4.7 REGULATORY CHANGE

Funding Standards

Regulatory issues facing private pension provision are common to other areas, for example regulation of the accountancy bodies. The issue of the adequacy of self-regulation for actuaries who are key professionals in advising pension schemes, has been examined by the Morris Inquiry in the UK (2005). The Morris inquiry notes extensive criticism of the actuarial profession in the UK, for example the failure to adopt the latest demographic techniques (p. 14) or the latest thinking from financial economics (p. 43). Problems were also identified with continuing professional development (p. 47-48) and the existence of conflicts of interest (p. 66). Similar issues are likely to arise within Ireland. The actuarial profession within Ireland is self regulated. The Society of Actuaries in Ireland is not an examining body. Membership is via successful completion of exams set by UK actuarial bodies (Society of Actuaries in Ireland, 2004). The Morris report made various recommendations, for example that actuaries in the UK should no longer be self regulated but rather regulated by the Financial Reporting Council – an independent body in the UK that also regulates accountants and the auditing industry.

One way in which regulators ensure that financial institutions are solvent is to require minimum ratios of assets to liabilities or prudent financial ratios. However, there are issues as to what are prudent financial ratios. In the case of banks, regulators focus on capital ratios – the ratio of own capital to total risk capital – and banks themselves may focus on a ratio referred to as 'value at risk'. In the case of pension funds of a defined benefit variety, regulators focus on a minimum funding standard which is based on an estimate of the value of benefits a scheme is obliged to pay (its liabilities) which should match the value of current assets. The adequacy of standards is not an issue if schemes are in surplus but comes into focus with projected deficits, for example due to poor investment returns or as a function of increased pension benefits coupled with a relatively high age profile of members. For example, a final salary defined benefit scheme that for a particular standard is in balance may move into deficit (independently of investment returns), depending on the rate of wage increase, the relative number of retired persons and if retirement patterns are grouped.

An important point to note is that there is a particular need for regulation in relation to pension provision. It is generally accepted that financial products need greater regulation than non-financial products because of their attributes – they are credence goods or belief goods. This means it is very difficult to assess the value of pension products because of their duration, because of the different amounts and quality of information held by employees, employers and financial institutions, and because of uncertainty.

Regulation of pension schemes in Ireland has concentrated on ensuring that minimum legal standards of operation, prudence and accountability are established and maintained. However, a particular problem has arisen in relation to ensuring pension funds meet the current actuarial standard. The problem is that many pension schemes do not meet the current standards and enforcing current standards may result in particularly adverse consequences. The Pensions Board (2004, p. 16) states: "It wishes to avoid a situation where regulatory requirements would cause otherwise viable pension schemes to close or change from their existing defined benefit basis".

The proposed solution is to introduce a new standard. This is a difficult task. A funding standard with "absolute security" would reflect "the market cost of replacing members benefits" (Pensions Board, 2004, p. 32). Such market costs are difficult to anticipate. Benefits to members of final salary-based occupational pension schemes are not actuarially fair. Risk arising from a known deficit may induce behaviour furthering increasing a deficit. This is because there are considerable cross subsidies. So that pensions in payment, and hence those employees with an option to retire, now have greater priority in the event of a scheme winding up. In the US, in the case of Kaiser Aluminium, pension scheme rules allowed retiring employees to withdraw lump sums, thus precipitating the collapse of the entire scheme (*New York Times*, December 18, 2003). Further cross subsidies that may affect funding adversely arise from wage increases which may involve a re-distribution, which is a function of the period of member-ship of the pension scheme. Such difficulties have been reported as being a particular issue in the case of negotiations between management and unions in the case of the ESB pension fund (*Irish Times*, September 11, 2004). Pensions scheme rules that may also involve cross subsidies relate to derived benefits (survivor pensions) so that a change in marital status automatically increases pension fund liabilities without any increase in contributions. Finally, there may also be cross subsidies arising from differential male/female longevity. So that the use of unisex actuarial tables helps ensure gender equality (as noted Council of the European Union, 2003, p. 37), but is at variance with a market based actuarially fair principle.

Further issues arise in rule setting because current rules

require the use of different criteria in estimating pension fund liabilities and pension fund assets. Current funding standards require employee pension liabilities to be estimated by discounting at an assumed rate of interest which is the yield on long dated government debt (Pensions Board, 2004, p. 38) and liabilities to current pensioners are calculated at the estimated market cost of purchasing an "equivalent annuity" (Pensions Board, 2004. p. 38). This means that as interest rates fall both estimated liabilities rise. Assets are valued for funding standard purposes at current market prices and asset prices but different asset classes do not behave in the same way in response to changes in interest rates. In particular, one class of assets equities (accounting for the bulk of pension fund assets) fell sharply in the period 2000-2002 while at the same time interest rates fell. One solution is to hold an asset class (government debt) whose price does reflect interest rate changes. Such an investment switch is described rather confusingly by the Pensions Board (2004, p. 27) as crystal-lizing "the underfunded position". A more consistent approach might be to discount flow of pension payments and estimated future flow of income from assets at the same rate. State welfare payments are currently more secure than private sector pension payments not because of adverse changes in asset values, but because GDP and flows of tax revenue have remained stable during recent periods of stock market volatility.

One suggested solution would be to replace a single number with a range of outcomes based on varying assumptions (Pensions Board, 2004, p. 18). This would have the advantage of drawing attention to pension scheme members and sponsors that forecasting is a subjective process. Another suggestion is that the discount rate be increased by using a combined return from government debt and equities (Pensions Board, 2004, p. 39). The Report does not, however, make clear what this equity rate is but there is an implicit assumption that it is a positive number which is larger than the current gilt rate.

An issue that arises from funding standards set by a regulator such as the Pensions Board is that they may result in different estimates of whether a pensions scheme is in surplus or deficit compared with accounting requirements (FRS 17) as monitored by the Irish Accounting and Auditing Supervisory Authority (IAASA). Under current Pension Board requirements, liabilities are discounted by the rate of interest on long-term government debt but under accounting requirements the rate of interest used is on AA rated corporate bonds resulting in a higher interest rate and reduced liabilities.

Other differences arise because the Pension Board relies on funding standards issued by the Society of Actuaries in Ireland as distinct from funding standards required in preparing company accounts (FRS 17). These differing standards cause divergences that may be positive or negative (Atherton, 2001, pp. 12-14). Difficulties with evaluating pension fund solvency arising from actuarial versus accounting standards are further compounded because companies producing published accounts will in future be required to use a further set of accounting standards, referred to as International Accounting Standards (IAS 19). There are numerous differences in the ways pension fund solvency may be estimated using FRS 17 compared with IAS 19. For example, the discount rate used is stated to be the yield on high quality corporate bonds or as an alternative the yields on government bonds (Ernst and Young GAAP 2005, p. 1693). In addition under IAS, gains or losses calculated using actuarial assumptions do not have to be incorporated immediately into published estimates of surplus or deficit (Ernst and Young GAAP 2005, p. 1696).

Whatever funding standard is adopted, a key assumption is that actuarial principles apply to occupational pensions, that pension rights are individually entitled

property rights and market based, rather than being collective and based on solidarity between all employees and employers, and on what is sometimes referred to as a 'pensions promise'. Actuarial standards are most appropriate where pensions are viewed as deferred pay, but are difficult to apply where there are considerable cross subsidies, between married and single people assuming pension benefits can be inherited, between those who are retired (or about to retire) and those at work (assuming pensions in payment have greater protection in the event of a pension fund deficit), and in the face of considerable uncertainty about future returns. Effectively, company pension schemes are more dependent on notions of solidarity between employers and employees, than would appear from an emphasis on funding and funding standards. Perhaps in view of these difficulties, the Social Welfare and Pensions Bill (2005) proposes relatively minor changes to funding standards.

A Pension Protection Scheme?

In 2003, the UK Government produced a Report (Simplicity, security and choice, 2003) setting out changes to the current UK 'voluntary system'. Amongst the recommendations was a proposal to improve protection of pension schemes so that "they would have greater confidence that they would benefit from their saving" (p. 1). This was to be achieved by establishing a Pension Protection Fund (p. 2); a reduced vesting period (that is, the minimum required period of working with a single employer to retain pension rights would be reduced to six months); and a new regulator (Department of Work and Pensions, 2002, p. 6; 2003, p. 15). The protection fund would be financed by a levy on schemes insured. The document states (p. 13, par. 7) "…under-funded schemes will pay a higher premium to the compensation fund compared with well-funded schemes. This risk based premium will be on top of a flat-rate levy payable by all employers with defined benefit schemes other than those public service schemes where benefits are guaranteed by government". The document recommends a new pensions regulator (p. 15) to focus on "tackling fraud, bad governance and poor adminis-tration" and a reduction in the level of indexation for defined benefit schemes to 2.5 per cent per annum (p. 23 par. 10).

The rationale given is as follows: "Improving the security of pension scheme benefits would ensure much greater confidence that pensions that have been promised would be delivered". The assumption is that if confidence is increased in eventual pension schemes a greater number of people will save more. A Pension Protection Fund was established in the UK under the Pensions Act, 2004, financed by a levy on all "private sector defined benefit or hybrid occupational schemes" (Source www.dwp. uk/lifeevent/, and administered by a new pensions regulator. In addition another scheme was established, referred to as a Financial Assistance Scheme, in order to pay compensation to members of existing insolvent pension schemes. Although the UK government committed £400 million to the scheme it has already been described as being far too low (*Financial Times*, November 10, 2004).

The establishment of an insurance fund to protect pension fund assets is also under consideration in Ireland (Pensions Board, 2004, p. 56). One important question to resolve is what should be insured? There are conflicting objectives with funded pension schemes: (1) to achieve maximum returns, and (2) as insurance or 'safety net' in old age. Part of this risk is the risk arising through higher than expected longevity. A major problem with the development of defined contribution schemes (money purchase plans) is that the investment returns objective is emphasised, with the possibility that assets are insufficient to fund a retirement pension. A pensions protection fund can insure against fraud (affecting a minority of schemes) but may not be able to insure against poor stock market returns (which may affect a majority of schemes). So that the Pensions Benefit Guarantee Corporation (PBGC) in the US had liabilities far in excess of assets in March 2003 (*Financial Times*, March 12, 2003) and as a result a pensions task force has been created in the US (*Financial Times*, August 30, 2004). The deficit of the PBGC is estimated at $11.2 billion (2004) and was expected to rise by $2.1 billion following the move of US Airways into Chapter 11 proceedings (*Financial Times*, September 14, 2004). In addition, a pensions protection fund will itself create further difficulties, for example moral hazard. The problem of adverse selection may also arise – those schemes with deficits or risky funds will join and will result in higher costs for all insured pension schemes. In the UK, despite the claimed benefits from insuring pension schemes, it is proposed that employers will be prevented from making compulsory membership of an occupational scheme a condition of employment (Department of Work and Pensions, 2003, p. 19).

Broaden the Scope of Regulation

With current and projected investment returns lower than in the past, costs of administering pension schemes and managing assets are more important. This requires a greater emphasis by the regulator on pension system costs and ensuring an efficient pension system. Evidence was presented earlier that the industry is not efficient in delivering income to pensioners. The Financial Services Authority in the UK has been extremely active in the pensions misselling controversy and in pension products described as 'with profits'. It would indeed be strange if similar issues did not exist in Ireland. In the case of Equitable Life, where it is estimated that there are 25,000-

30,000 policyholders resident within Ireland, merely representations (rather than investigations) were conducted on their behalf by The Irish Financial Services Regulatory Authority [1].

Merge Regulators?

Part of the solution to the pensions 'crisis' in the UK is to change the regulatory regime. The structure of the current Irish regulatory regime has considerable advantages in that it is representative of the pensions industry and other interested parties. This allows for access to considerable private sector expertise, but there is also a danger that it may be less responsive to consumer interests.

Pension products and services are provided by multi-sector financial firms. With the growth of individual pension plans and inheritance rights to streams of payment and lump sums in some cases, the difference between pension plans and savings schemes has become much more blurred. Many aspects of financial firms' activities are regulated by the Irish Financial Services Regulatory Authority (IFSRA), with the exception of pensions. This is an anomaly and the commitment to seek a 'memorandum of understanding' with the IFSRA (Pension Board Annual Report, 2004) is to be welcomed. The McDowell Report (1999, par. 3.17) had recommended "that there should be a structured approach to co-operation between the Pensions Board" and the new regulatory Authority, but this was not provided for in legislation establishing the Financial Services Regulatory Authority (Central Bank and Financial Services Act 2003). There is a danger that systemic failures would require considerable regulatory resources in order to pursue proactive policies (such as investigations of pension misselling) or to investigate problems with pension policies described as 'with profit' (as in the UK). One solution is a full merger with IFSRA, while retaining valuable input from professionals and the industry in order to focus on the key function of a pension system which is to provide pension income to those in retirement. To be effective this solution would also require a more proactive financial regulatory regime by IFSRA than appears to currently exist (see for example John McManus, *Irish Times*, November 15, 2004).

4.9 CONCLUSION

With recent stock market volatility, even with the growth of personal retirement plans, it is likely that the State old age pension will remain the primary source of income to future retired persons (Connell and Stewart, 2004). In most economies where stock markets have fallen by up to 50 per cent in 2000-2002, GDP growth has remained reasonably stable. Hence, Government tax revenues and the ability to finance social welfare pensions (and pensions of public sector employees) have not been affected as adversely as private sector pension arrangements.

However, there is no debate about the importance of the private sector pension system, particularly in Ireland, and, for example, the UK and the Netherlands. A substantial fraction of the labour force is dependent on the private sector pension system to deliver pension income. The pension system plays a key role in the allocation of savings. But the pension system also attracts considerable tax relief and, given the relatively low flows of income from occupational pension schemes compared with the State scheme, the question must be raised as to whether these tax expenditures are good value for money? One way of considering such expenditures is that tax payers in general are exposed to risk through stock market volatility. If pension funds experience poor returns, consumption and economic growth will be reduced, apart from welfare losses to future retirees. If we assume that society is unlikely to allow widespread poverty in old age, a collapse in sources of pension income from funded pension schemes is likely to be compensated (at least partly) by increased State expenditures. A pension scheme insurance fund with ultimate liabilities guaranteed by the State could be interpreted as a formalisation of this implicit contract and involves further risk sharing with taxpayers in general, that is, with society as a whole.

In a future investment environment characterised by low returns and low interest rates, accumulating a lump sum over a 40 year period to fund a pension over 20 or more years which replaces half or two-thirds of pre-retirement earnings is likely to be beyond the resources of most people. We have noted that currently most people are dependent on the State old age pension for retirement income; that the size of the 'savings gap' is highly dependent on the level of State old age pensions. We have also noted that with integration an increase in the level of the State old age pension would reduce pension scheme deficits.

The next chapter considers in greater detail the current and possible future role of the State in pension provision.

Notes

1. In response to complaints from Irish resident policyholders of Equitable Life, the Irish Financial Services Regulatory Authority (IFSRA) merely wrote to the Financial Services Compensation Scheme (FSCS) in the UK. Source http://www.ifsra.ie, news release, August 23, 2004.

References

Atherton, J. (2001), A Users Guide to FRS 17, The Stable Inn Actuarial Society, paper given to the Society of Actuaries in Ireland, November 28, 2001.

Bodie, Z. and R. Merton (1998), *Finance*, Prentice-Hall: New Jersey.

Central Statistics Office (2004a), Quarterly National Household Survey Pensions Update, Quarter 1 2004, September 2004.

Central Statistics Office (2004b), Quarterly National Household Survey Pensions Update, Quarter 3 2004, December 2004.

Concialdi, P. and A. Lechevalier (2003), "Intergenerational Equity and Pension Reform", Chapter 12, in Hughes G. and Stewart J. (eds.) *Reforming Pensions in Europe: Evolution of Pension Financing and Sources of Retirement Income,* Cheltenham: Edward Elgar.

Connell, P. and J. Stewart (2003), Income of Retired Persons in Ireland: Some Evidence from Household Budget Surveys" in Hughes, G. and J. Stewart (eds.) *Reforming Pensions in Europe: Evolution of Pension Financing and Sources of Retirement Income,* Cheltenham: Edward Elgar.

Council of the European Union (2003), Draft Joint Report by the Commission and the Council on adequate and sustainable pensions, 6527/1/03, Brussels: Council of the European Union, available at http://europa. eu.int/comm/employment.

Davies, B. (2000), "Equity Within and Between Generations: Pension Systems and Equity", in Hughes, G. and J. Stewart (eds.) *Pensions in the European Union: Adapting to Economic and Social Change*, London: Kluwer Academic Publishers.

Davis, G. (1999), "Dangers in Government Plan to Provide for Pensioners of Future", *Irish Times*, 18 August 1999.

Davis, E.P. (1995), *Pension Funds Retirement – Income Security and Capital Markets*, Oxford: Clarendon Press.

Department of Finance (2000), *Commission on Public Sector Pensions Final Report*, pn. 9209, Dublin: Stationery Office.

Department of Work and Pensions (2003), *Simplicity, Security and Choice: Working and Saving for Retirement, Action on occupational pensions*, London: H.M.S.O. Cm 5835.

Department of Work and Pensions (2002), *Simplicity, Security and Choice: Working and Saving for Retirement*, London: Stationery Office, Cm 5677, available at http://www.dwp.gov.uk.

Dimson, E., P. Marsh and M. Staunton (2002), *Triumph of the Optimists 101 Years of Global Investment Returns*, Princeton: Princeton University Press.

Doyle, N. (2004) Closing the Gap, New Policy Proposals, Irish Insurance Federation.

Ernst and Young (2004), *International GAAP 2005*, London: Ernst and Young.

European Commission (1999), Financial Services: Implementing the Framework for Financial Markets: Action Plan, Co. (1999) 232, 11.05.99.

Financial Committee (2002), Report by the Economic and Financial Committee (EFC) on EU financial integration, *European Economy*, no. 171.

Government Actuaries Department (2003), Occupational Schemes, 2000, Eleventh Survey by the Governments Actuary Department, available at http://www.gad.gov.uk/Publications/.

Green Paper (2002), *Simplicity, Security and Choice: Working and Saving for Retirement*, London: Stationery Office, Cm 5677, December 2002.

Hughes, G. (1996), "Would Privatising Pensions Increase Savings?", *Irish Banking Review*, Spring 1996.

Hughes, G. and B. J. Whelan (1996), *Occupational and Personal Pension Coverage 1995*, Dublin: Economic and Social Research Institute.

Irish Financial Services Regulatory Authority (2005), "Review of Remunerations Structures and Transparency", Dublin: Irish Financial Services Regulatory Authority.

Kehoe, James R. (2003), Pension Provision in Ireland – The Shape of Things to Come, Dublin: Marsh & McLennan.

Lane, Clark & Peacock (2004), Accounting for Pensions, available at www.lcp.uk.com.

Life Strategies (2004), Quantifying the Retirement Savings Shortfall, Dublin: Irish Insurance Federation.

McDowell Report (1999), *Report of the Implementation Advisory Group on the Establishment of a Single Regulatory Authority for the Financial Services Sector*, Dublin: Department of Finance, Pn 7271.

Miles, D. (1977), "Financial Markets, Ageing and Social Welfare", *Fiscal Studies*, vol. 18, no. 2, pp. 161-187.

Morris Review (2005), Morris Review of the Actuarial Profession, Final Report, London: H.M.S.O., available at: http://www.hm-treasury.gov.uk.

Myners Report, (2001), *Institutional Investment in the UK: A Review*, London: H.M. Treasury, available at http://www.hm-treasury.gov.uk/.

National Academy of Social Insurance (1998), "Report of the Panel on Privatization of Social Security", Washington: National Academy of Social Insurance, available at http://www.nasi.org.

Observatoire des Retraites (2004), Pension in the European Union, *La Lettre de l'Observatoire des Retraites*, October 2004, no. 13.

Pensions Board (1998), *Securing Retirement Income, National Pensions Policy Initiative*, Dublin: Pensions Board.

Pensions Board (2003), Personal Retirement Savings Accounts (PRSAs), Frequently Asked Questions, Dublin: Pensions Board available at http://www.pensionsboard.ie/.

Pensions Board (2004), Consultation Document on Review

of the Funding Standard, Dublin: Pensions Board, available at http://www.pensionsboard.ie/.

Pensions Commission (2004), *Pensions: Challenges and Choices: The First Report of the Pensions Commission*, London: Stationery Office, available at www.pensionscommission.org.uk.

Society of Actuaries in Ireland (2003), Position Paper on Defined Contribution Plans & PRSA, Dublin: Society of Actuaries.

Society of Actuaries in Ireland (2004), An Overview of the Actuarial Profession in Ireland, Dublin: Society of Actuaries, available at available at: http://www.hm-treasury.gov.uk.

Stewart, J. and B. McNally (2003), "Occupational Pension Schemes in Ireland – A Review of Risk and Investment Strategies", paper given at the Irish Accounting and Finance Association Conference, 15.5.03.

Stewart, J. (1996), "Pension Funds As Shareholders", in Emmanuel Reynaud et al. *International Perspectives on Supplementary Pensions*, London: Quorum Books, pp. 207-20.

World Bank, (1994), *Averting the Old Age Crisis*, Oxford: Oxford University Press.

Chapter 5

The State Pension – Towards a Basic Income for the Elderly?*

BY ANTHONY MCCASHIN

INTRODUCTION

This chapter deals with State social security pensions –'social welfare pensions' in popular parlance. These pensions provide the sole source of income for a substantial segment of the older population, and totalled about €2.4 billions in 2003 (2.2 per cent of GNP). Aside from their significance for the older, low-income population, they underpin the structure of many private sector occupational pensions, as the design and funding of these pensions is predicated on their members' participation in the State's social insurance system and receipt of a State social insurance pension. Furthermore, as the projected ageing of the Irish population gets underway (see Chapter 3), the size of the social welfare recipient population will grow both absolutely and as a share of the population.

*   The author acknowledges the permission of Gill and MacMillan publishers to reproduce material from chapter 10, *Social Security in Ireland* (2004) in the historical background section.

Other chapters bring into sharp focus the limitations of the current pensions system: the coverage of the occupational pensions sector (outside of State and quasi-State employments) remains low; the costs of the tax supports underpinning occupational pensions have escalated and now rival those of the direct State social welfare pensions; these tax reliefs are regressive, being of disproportionate benefit to employees on higher incomes; and, the recently introduced Personal Retirement Savings Accounts (PRSAs) are unlikely to substantially increase private pensions coverage among people on lower incomes.

Against this background, the present chapter argues that there is a need to strengthen the State social security system and enhance its role in the overall pensions structure. Briefly, the argument is that a simpler, considerably more comprehensive State pension is at the heart of a more effective and equitable pension system. First, however, it is useful to take a brief overview of the development of the State pension – this is done in the next section. Then Section 5.2 gives a brief description of the current arrangements and some recent trends. The core of the chapter is contained in Sections 5.3 and 5.4, which highlight some limitations of current provisions and offer a new perspective on how these might be addressed. Section 5.5 considers some of the complexities and transition problems in changing this part of the pensions system along the lines advocated here.

5.1 HISTORICAL BACKGROUND

The first phase in the evolution of State old age pensions commenced in 1908 when the reforming Liberal government in London provided for pensions in the UK and Ireland for all persons aged 70 years and over, subject to a means test and to proof of non-imprisonment and non-receipt of Poor Relief in a specified period. The pension, later to be re-named the Old Age Non-contributory Pension (OANCP), came into effect in 1909 in Ireland and the UK and was especially popular in Ireland for two reasons. First, as the amount of the pension was set with the incomes and living costs of British urban workers in mind, it comprised a high proportion of the earnings of Irish labourers and agricultural workers. Second, the pension offered older persons an alternative to the dreaded prospect of institutionalisation in a Poor Law Workhouse.

From the time of its introduction until political independence some modifications were made to the pension. The residency requirement of 20 years was relaxed and the exclusion of former Poor Relief recipients was abolished. More significantly, the Blind Persons Act of 1920 extended the pension to blind persons aged 50 and over, and the rate of pension was doubled. However, the new Free State Government inherited the original structure of the pension. At the time of its introduction, nationalist politicians had been very aware of the costs of the pension. This awareness, combined with a continuing unease about applicants' ability to provide documentary proof of age, may have contributed to the government's willingness to use the pension as a source of economies in the 1924 budget. In the budget the maximum rate of pension was reduced by 10 per cent and the means test was tightened. As a result, the total number of pensions fell and the number of maximum pensions in payment fell sharply.

The reduction in the pension was restored in 1928, but pensions had become highly politicised and became "something of a defining issue between Fianna Fail and Cumann na nGaedheal" (O Grada, 2002: p.155). The pension featured as an election issue in 1932 (and again in 1933) and early in the life of the Fianna Fail government important changes were made to the old age pension:

- The 'benefit and privilege' clause taking account of the

means of resident family members was abolished;
- The bar on elected representatives making representations about pension applications was removed;
- The Poor Relief disqualification was finally abolished;
- The age of qualification for blind persons was reduced to 30 from 50.

In the 1930s and 1940s, the pension became less politically contentious, as governments administered pensions legislation more leniently. Also, proof of age was no longer problematic from the mid-1930s, removing one of the bones of contention and one source of appeals against refusal of applications. Pensions were integrated with the newly introduced provision for widows in the late 1930s, so that a widow in receipt of a contributory pension at age 70 would become entitled, irrespective of means, to a maximum old age pension. The final significant act in the early development of the pensions was the legislation of 1951 allowing some farmers to assign their farm to their children without affecting the right to a pension. This change and other changes to the means test for blind persons' pensions were brought in by the Inter-Party government (1948-1951) as part of its attempt to secure political support for the wider social security plan outlined in the 1949 White Paper, *Social Security*. The White Paper proposed a comprehensive national social insurance system, similar to that proposed in the landmark Beveridge Report in the UK and implemented there in 1946 (Beveridge, 1942). One element of this comprehensive scheme was to be a State social insurance pension. The White Paper gave rise to the consolidating legislation in the 1952 Social Welfare Act, but this reform did not include a State social insurance pension.

A new phase in the development of pensions began with the 1960 Social Welfare Act, which legislated for the introduction of a social insurance pension, the Old Age

Contributory Pension (OACP). Coverage of the OACP was confined to persons insured under the social security legislation, thereby excluding the self-employed, public servants and people above the income limit for social insurance contributions. From the early 1960s until the early 1980s, pensions developed within the framework of the OACP and the OANCP. In the 1970s, the pace of change quickened, reflecting in part the emphasis on social security issues of the 1973-1977 Labour-Fine Gael coalition government. A Retirement Pension (RP) was introduced in 1970 and then, in rapid succession during the years of Coalition government, the age of eligibility was reduced from 70 to 66 for the OACP and the OANCP and 65 for the RP. The long-term potential pool of social insurance pensioners also expanded with the abolition of the income ceiling for contributors to social insurance.

In the mid-1970s, the policy debate changed. The first official contribution to this new debate was the Green Paper, *A National Income Related Pension Scheme* (Department of Social Welfare, 1976). This came in the wake of significant real improvements in the value of the OACP and OANCP and a reduction in the age of eligibility for these pensions, and the momentum towards extension and development of the State pension system was strong at that time.

The Green Paper identified these shortcomings in the pensions system: inadequate coverage of occupational pensions among both employees and the self-employed; exclusion of the self-employed from social insurance; lack of protection of pension rights for members of occupational schemes; the absence of an income replacement element; and, uncertain and mixed arrangements about indexation of pensions. It started, not only from a pragmatic recognition of the deficiencies of the current arrangements, but also with an explicit preference for income-related rather than flat-rate pensions (Department of Social Welfare, 1976, p. 62):

Fundamentally what is needed is the basing of the
pensions to be provided in a national system on the
concept that pension is in replacement of lost income or
earnings and should, therefore, be related to the level of
such income or earnings.

Having offered this argument in favour of an income-
related pension, the Green Paper set out a number of
versions of an income-related pension system and gave
illustrations of pension levels along with forecasts of their
budgetary costs and contribution requirements. It also
offered a review of the arguments about how pensions
should be funded, whether on a pay-as-you-go (PAYG) or
funded basis (with contribution income being set aside into
a fund from which future pension liabilities will be met).
The Green Paper was ambivalent. On the one hand, it fully
acknowledged the deficiencies of the contemporary system
and firmly argued for a State income-related pension. This,
combined with the detail it offered of possible new designs
and their cost and contribution requirements, implied that
at the time the government might be strongly disposed
towards an income-related pension. On the other hand, it
explicitly pointed out that the analysis of costs in no way
implied a decision to advocate an income-related pension. It
also outlined what it saw as the potentially negative
consequences of higher (pension) contribution rates on
employers and employees, and argued that an expanded
pension system based on PAYG principles could displace
national savings and investment.

There was considerable public and political interest in
the policy issues raised in the Green Paper, although an
income-related pension was not introduced. A White Paper
on the topic was drafted but never published, and by the
early 1980s, the prospect of income-related pensions had
receded from public and political view. In fact, policy
developed in an entirely different direction. After the Green

Paper was published, the existing social security pensions were further improved (further lowering of the pension age and increases in the real value of the payments) and a further Green Paper *Social Insurance for the Self Employed* was published (Department of Social Welfare, 1978). In the early 1980s the economy entered a period of rising unemployment and escalating levels of national debt. There was a change of government in 1977 and further changes in 1981, and again in January 1982 and November 1982. A Labour-Fine Gael coalition government took office in 1982 and the Labour party was again assigned responsibility for social security. However, a new twist was put on pensions policy in the early 1980s when the lack of regulation in occupational pensions led to some widely publicised crises of standards, funding and accountability. Taken together, these new circumstances led to a decisive shift in the focus of public policy.

In 1985, the then Minister for Social Welfare publicly outlined the likely development of pensions in the future, suggesting that the priority issues were: the social insurance coverage of the self-employed; the need for regulation of occupational pensions; and the necessity to sustain the value of the existing State pensions. In relation to income related pensions, the Minister stated that (Minister for Social Welfare, 1985, p.16)

> The main emphasis in the State scheme will have to remain on aiming to ensure that flat-rate pensions achieve a reasonable relationship with earnings. That is not to say that the issue of pay-related pensions can or will be ignored. But the options there have to be considered in terms of what the economy can afford at a time when the overriding priority is unemployment.

The Minister then announced (in the same speech) the establishment of a National Pensions Board (NPB) and outlined the proposed Board's terms of reference. Quite independently of the emergence of the NPB, the Commission on Social Welfare offered an overview of pensions and of social insurance more generally. The Commission broadly concurred with the Green Paper's analysis of the deficiencies of the pensions system and welcomed the establishment of the NPB. It suggested that an earnings-related pension was not a priority and that the main objective of policy "should be to use limited resources to improve the income position of all categories of social welfare recipients" (Commission on Social Welfare, 1986, p. 328).

The establishment of the NPB in 1986 ushered in the third and most recent phase in the evolution of pensions. Policy moved quickly from the mid-1980s onwards, with the NPB producing a succession of reports that fed directly into policy (NPB, 1987; NPB, 1988; NPB, 1993; NPB 1998). In 1989, the self-employed were included in the social insurance system: this development followed the recommendations of both the NPB's (1988) report on the subject and the Commission on Social Welfare's report. Then, in 1990, the Pensions Act was passed, and became law in 1991. Here the legislation followed closely the NPB's reports on the regulation of occupational pensions and the implementation of the EU's Equal Treatment Directive as it pertained to occupational pensions. Briefly, the Pensions Act put the NPB on a statutory footing as the overarching regulatory and advisory body, and constructed a new legislative framework for occupational pensions, setting out detailed legislation about funding standards, the roles of pension trustees, the rights of pension fund members, and so on.

These reforms, however, were only part of the wider pensions system for which the NPB was given policy responsibility. In 1993, the NPB (1993) issued its final report, *Developing the National Pension System*, giving detailed recommendations about all aspects of the pensions system but, more importantly, offering a view about the long-standing question of income-related pensions. The majority of the NPB did not agree that there should be a State income-related pension and the Board recommended that "the coverage of occupational schemes and personal pension arrangements should continue to be encouraged, in particular the existing tax treatment should be encouraged" (NPB, 1993, p. 202). Also, the NPB repudiated the idea of compulsory second-tier pensions, whether in *a State scheme or compulsory occupational and private pensions.* However, there were familiar lines of disagreement. The Trade Unions expressed a preference for State income-related pensions funded by additional percentage PRSI deductions, while business and employer interests expressed opposition to compulsory income related pensions "under any circumstances" (NPB, p. 203).

The NPB's final report sparked further policy debate, the first round in which was the official publication, *National Pensions Policy Initiative: Consultation Document* (Department of Social Welfare, 1997). In this document the government and the NPB jointly attempted to stimulate debate on the overall structure of pensions provision in Ireland, and raised again the fundamental questions that had driven policy debate since the 1970s Green Paper, questions such as the role of the State in pensions provision, the desirability of an income-related pension, and the possibility of compulsory occupational coverage. The consultation document set out broad policy options, reviewed some relevant international experience, and listed relevant policy criteria. However, while the discussion in the consultation document was studiously neutral, the stances already expressed by the various interests in the NPB's 1993 report were firmly re-stated: the trade unions advocated a role for a State income-related pension, and the business and employer organisations expressed opposition to any obligatory second-tier pension.

The key point in the consultation document was the NPB's separate statement of its preferred policy. This statement reiterated in full the view the NPB had outlined in its 1993 report (Department of Social Welfare, 1997, p. 59):

> The Board concluded that, having regard to existing levels of coverage, international experience and the number of small employers in Ireland, it is highly unlikely that comprehensive pension cover, which would maintain established standards of living, can be achieved under the present national pension system (compulsory social insurance for flat-rate pensions and voluntary occupational or personal pension arrangements providing supplementary pension cover).

The Board also had serious reservations as to whether a second-tier, income-related pension scheme under social insurance would be sustainable in the longer term, in the light of the demographic projections and the projected level of contributions required just to finance first-tier social insurance pensions. Accordingly, the key elements in the NPB's strategy are:

- Occupational pensions (under the regime introduced in the 1990 Act) to remain voluntary and supported through extensive tax reliefs;

- A new form of private pension, Personal Retirement Savings Accounts (PRSAs) to be introduced, regulated by the Pensions Board, and incentivised by tax reliefs;

- The State social welfare pension to remain as a flat-rate pension, within a framework of indexation that would lead to a pension level of 34per cent of gross average earnings.

In summary, Ireland's State old age pensions system now

comprises a means-tested social assistance pension (Non-Contributory) and a social insurance pension (Contributory). The age of eligibility for both pensions is 66, although there is a separate Retirement Pension (RP) payable at age 65 for which there are more rigorous contribution requirements. This is the first tier of Ireland's pension system: it co-exists alongside separate pension provisions for civil servants and other public servants, occupational pensions for private sector employees, and newly introduced Personal Retirement Savings Accounts (PRSAs). The next section offers further detail about the current State pensions and summarises some recent trends.

5.2 STATE PENSIONS – AN OVERVIEW

Table 5.1 below summarises the key data. In 2003, there were 288,000 State old age pension recipients in all, and expenditure totalled in excess of €2.4 billions, or 2.2 percent of GNP: the bulk of this is attributable to the OACP and RP.

Table 5.1. Old Age Pensions – Number of Recipients and Expenditure in 2003

Pension	Recipients (000s)	Expenditure (€m)	Expenditure per cent
Contributory	114	947	39
Retirement	87	899	37
Non-contributory	87	565	23
All	288	2,411	100

Source: *Statistical Information on Social Welfare Services 2003*, Department of Social and Family Affairs.

Briefly, the *Contributory pension* is payable at age 66 based on applicant's social insurance record. It is not conditional on retirement. For those reaching age 66 from 2002[1] onwards the principle contribution requirements are as follows:

commencement of social insurance contributions before reaching 56 years of age; at least 260 (full-rate) contributions paid; and a yearly average of at least 48 (full-rate) contributions paid (or credited) from 1979 to the end of the tax year before reaching 66, or a yearly average of at least 10 (paid or credited) from 1953 (or, if later, the year insurable employment commenced). The amount of pension payable is tiered according to the social insurance profile: to receive the maximum pension the yearly average number of contribution is 48, and for the minimum pension, 10 contributions.

In assessing social insurance records, 'credited' contributions can be included. Important examples of these include periods of unemployment and sickness when unemployment and disability benefit are being paid. Also, years spent working in the home are disregarded when calculating the yearly average contribution figure. Specifically, years spent in the home since 1994 caring for children up to age six (increased to age 12 in 1995) are disregarded in this way – up to a maximum of 20 years. This provision, which also applies to those caring for incapacitated persons, has the effect of indirectly supplementing the social insurance record of those carers and people (overwhelmingly women) who have spent long periods out of the labour force.

Turning to the *Retirement Pension*, the contribution rules are similar to those of the OACP. Here, however, there is a retirement pre-condition and the pension is payable at age 65. At age 66, the retirement condition ceases. As in the case of the OACP, the amount of the pension is tiered according to the yearly average number of contributions.[2]

The *Non-contributory Pension* is means-tested and the age of eligibility is 66. The means test takes account of a spouse's income and includes earnings, interest on savings and capital, income from property, and so on. However, the value of a pensioner's home is not included where the pensioner is resident, and the first €12,500 of capital is disregarded in estimating interest income.[3]

Finally, it is important to note that in common with all other benefits and allowances, additional amounts are paid in respect of adult dependants and child dependants of all pensioners, in the case of all three pensions. Pensions are supplemented in two other ways: an age supplement is payable for those aged over 80 and there is a further allowance for those living alone.

Table 5.2. Recent Trends in State pensions

Pension	1994	2004
Population age 65+ as per cent of Total	11.5	11.1
No. of State pensioners (000s)	241	288
Pensioners as per cent of Pop. 65+	59	67
Insurance pensions as per cent of Total	55	70
Percent of Men 65+ in receipt of OACP/RP	52.4	71.4
Percent of Women 65+ in receipt of OACP/RP	23	27
OACP as per cent of Net Earnings	39.7	36.4
Total Pensions Expenditure as per cent of GNP	2.7	2.2

Source: Department of Social and Family Affairs, Central Statistics Office.
Notes: The years to which the data refer may vary within a year or two of 1994

Table 5.2 above summarises some key trends in relation to these pensions in the last decade. As the data shows, the share of older persons in the population declined slightly. However, both the number of pensioners and the percent of older persons in receipt of a pension have risen significantly. There has also been a shift in the composition of pensioners towards the insurance-based pensions. There is also a clear gender pattern among pension recipients – women are less likely to be recipients of a social insurance pension than men. The critical revelation in the table is the link between the pension and net earnings i.e. the income replacement rate. This *fell* during the last decade or so, reflecting the fact that although the pension was incrementally increasing in real (i.e. inflation-adjusted) terms, it declined relative to the rapidly rising incomes in the economy as a whole.

The final row of the table shows the net outcome of these inter-related trends. Pensions expenditure fell as a share of national income. In 1991, expenditure was 3.0 per cent of GNP, by 1994 it was 2.7, and it currently stands at 2.2 per cent.

Figure 5.1 Pensioner Poverty

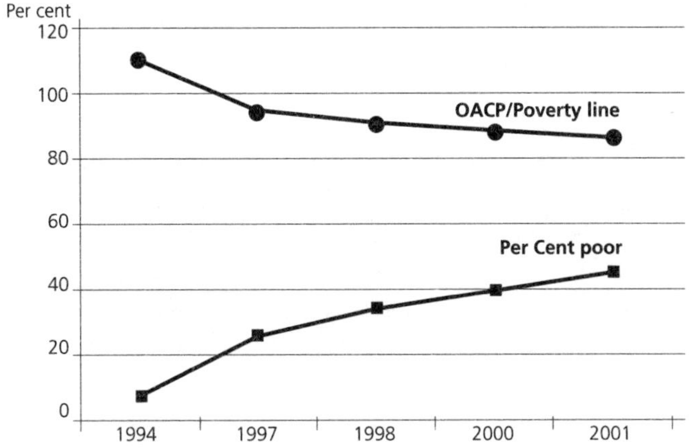

Source: McCashin (2004), Whelan et al (2003).

Figure 5.1 brings out the implication of the trends in pension levels: poverty among the older population rose when measured in relative income terms. The chart shows, first, trends in the ratio of the OACP to the poverty line, which is half of average net disposable income. As incomes rose generally, the poverty line also rose: while pension levels increased (and actually increased more than prices), they did not keep pace with net incomes. The corollary was a rise in pensioner poverty using this relative income measure. The first series in the figure gives the value of the

OACP as per cent of a relative income poverty line – in this case, the line is half of median income. Over time this figure has declined markedly, and in combination with the growth in reliance on this pension, this resulted in a sharp increase in poverty among pensioners. In 2001, over 44 per cent of persons aged 65 or over had an income below 60 per cent of median income.

The more recent data on poverty for 2003 in the official *Survey of Income and Living Conditions* confirms the high rate of poverty among older persons: 36.4 per cent of persons aged 65 or over were at risk of poverty compared with 22.7 per cent for the population as a whole, and for females in this age group the figure is over 40 per cent (CSO, 2005).

5.3 ISSUES AND PROBLEMS

The pattern recorded in the figures above is familiar to commentators on poverty trends in Ireland and illustrates a general trend (McCashin, 2004, p. 69; Whelan, Layte *et al*, 2003). Over the last decade or so, as incomes in the economy soared and tax rates were reduced, the level of benefits and allowances fell relative to net incomes, and poverty among social security recipients (in a relative income sense) increased. However, unlike other categories of benefit recipients, many pensioners rely on the pension on a long-term basis as their sole source of income. The implication of these trends for social policy and, in partic-ular, for anti-poverty policy have been widely discussed and are not dealt with here.

The trend of rising poverty among the elderly provides strong grounds for reconsidering pension provisions, but a focus on this issue in isolation from a broader analysis would limit the discussion exclusively to the level of the State pension. Poverty prevention among the elderly, while clearly an important policy objective, is not the only one. Other policies are relevant too: encouragement of saving for retirement; equalising the incomes of men and women; facilitating the social and economic participation of older persons; achieving some degree of income replacement; and the redistribution of income. Viewed in this broader way, a series of issues arise about the pension system.

Considering State pensions first, the current arrangements are highly complex, comprising a range of very detailed rules about contribution conditions and means tests for the contributory and non-contributory pensions respectively[4]. Complexity imposes costs, however indirect, on both claimant and administrator alike. However, a more important question about this complexity is the uncertainty it may create for individuals about their future entitlements and the consequence this may have for their savings strategies. For example, it is not clear what impact the means test for the non-contributory pension might have on the savings behaviour of prospective retirees. Arguably, it may reduce their incentive to save, either because they misunderstand the means test, or fear that future changes in the means test will result in a lower pension or exclusion from the pension.

This has implications, too, for the official policy of encouraging retirement saving through PRSAs introduced by the NPB. Employees with incomplete social insurance histories (for example, late entrants or re-entrants to the workforce) are less likely to qualify for a full OACP, and if they are on a low income or in insecure employment they are less likely to have an occupational pension. These are the categories of worker for whom the means-tested NCOAP is a fallback and for whom the new PRSA provisions are intended. However, the means test for the NCOAP (or perceptions of it) may deter such people from embarking on a PRSA scheme.

A further complexity is the way in which the concept of adult dependant is operationalised in the State pensions and other social security benefits. The benefits system, as noted earlier, is structured around a personal rate of payment and an Additional Adult 'Dependant' payment for those with spouses. Child Dependant Additions may also be payable. In the gender-neutral rules that now apply, the additional payment is paid subject to the income of the 'dependant'. Briefly, a pensioner whose partner has no income would be entitled to an addition; so, too, would a pensioner whose spouse's income was below a threshold. Those whose spouses had an income above the threshold would receive a reduced payment for the spouse, or none, according to a tiered system of payments. This compounds the complexity and uncertainty. Furthermore, as these arrangements apply to both the insurance (OACP) and the means-tested (NCOAP) assistance pension, they introduce, albeit indirectly, a significant element of means testing into the social insurance system. The question of employment incentives also arises here. The 'dependant' rule may act as a disincentive to older spouses to take up paid work, as this affects the pensions partners receive.

On a wider front, the achievement of gender equality is a generally accepted aim of public policy. The social security system has been one of the areas of public policy in which contentious and complex changes have been made to overturn the historic discrimination against women in the social security system (McCashin, 2004, Chapter 6). Formally, social security is now gender neutral. However, in the area of pensions, the system does not result in equal outcomes for men and women in one important respect: married women are less likely to secure independent pensions. For example, they are much less likely to receive non-means tested pensions than men. This is due to the different labour market trajectories of men and women: women who spend long periods out of paid employment will have inferior social insurance contribution records. The arrangements introduced in the mid-1990s ameliorate this to some extent, as time spent on domestic caring duties is now disregarded in calculating the average yearly number of social insurance contributions. At best, this is an indirect and limited recognition of care work and insufficient to put women with substantial histories of care work on an equal footing with men (Murphy, 2003).

Both men and women are eligible to apply for the non-contributory pension. Here, too, in a context of formal gender equality, married women may be less likely to achieve separate pensions, because of the aggregation of spouses' incomes in the means test. Spouses may receive additional adult payments for their partners as 'dependants', as noted earlier, but a strong case can be made that in old age women pensioners should be treated as independent adults.

Turning to the link between State pensions and the wider pensions system, two points should be noted. The first of these is the tax treatment of occupational pensions: these are increasingly costly and of disproportionate benefit to those on higher incomes. Gerard Hughes deals with this issue in detail in Chapter 6. Here it is important to note that the substantial revenue foregone on the tax treatment of occupational pensions imposes a significant opportunity cost: some of the tax expenditures could be re-allocated to improve the level of the State old age pensions. Second, a significant proportion of occupational pensions are integrated, broadly in these terms. The formula governing the pensionable salary takes account of the State pension, for example, pensionable salary may be defined as gross basic pay minus 1.5 times the OACP. The effect of this is to create a form of 'poverty trap' whereby substantial increases in the State pension may result in a reduced occupational pension. Equally, this form of integration can mean that some low paid employees, having contributed to an occupational pension, find that the integration formula (pay minus State pension = pensionable income) results in a negligible occupational pension.

5.4 A NEW APPROACH?

At this point, it is useful to place the pensions system and its problems in the context of recent debates about the social security and tax system more generally, specifically the debate whether the entire benefit system should be replaced by a simple, universal, integrated system. Such integrated systems come in many forms, but the one that has occasioned most debate in Ireland is Basic Income (BI), alternatively titled Citizen's Income, or Social Dividend. What is Basic Income, why has it been advocated and how is it relevant to the improvement of the pension system?

Basic Income is one variant of what the analytical policy literature refers to as an Integrated Tax and Benefit system. The specific form of BI that has been advocated and debated entails, simply, a fundamental repudiation of the current social insurance and social system and a sweeping reform of the personal income tax system. These are the key components of a BI scheme: -

- All adults (say 18 years of age and over) are paid an unconditional weekly income – no means test or insurance contributions;
- An unconditional payment is also made in respect of all dependent children (those under 18); and

- All personal income – excluding the BI – is taxed at one rate without any tax allowances or credits of any kind, and some variants of BI also entail the abolition of employers' or employees' social insurance contributions, or both.

At the level of an individual, net income, Y, under these arrangements can be expressed as: $Y = BI + (E - tE)$, where is E is earnings and t is the tax rate. On the benefits side, this system entails the outright abolition of the categorical social insurance and assistance payments and their associated contribution requirements, means tests, and other eligibility criteria. In the case of taxation, it reduces the tax rate structure to one single proportional tax rate and simplifies the tax structure through the elimination of all tax allowances.

Why has such a reform been advocated in Ireland and elsewhere? BI has been advanced from a variety of political and policy stances, but the common threads running through the demand for BI-type schemes are as follows. In the first instance, it is argued that social insurance and assistance schemes are complex and cumbersome and require the State to monitor the status of recipients and applicants – to ensure they are unemployed if they are in receipt of unemployment benefit, to insist that lone parents are not, in fact, cohabiting with partners, and so on. BI schemes, in contrast, are simple and non-bureaucratic. Second, a feature of many proposed BI schemes is their focus on individuals. In pure versions of BI, the payment is made unconditionally to all adults without reference to gender, marital status, household status or other such criteria. Therefore, its advocates argue, BI offers a way of structuring the benefit system that is consistent with contemporary patterns of household formation, family patterns and so on. There would be no need under BI to distinguish categories such as married, single, lone parent, carer, or dependant. Quite simply, a payment is made universally and unconditionally to all citizens.

Third, social insurance systems are invariably complemented by means-tested social assistance. Proponents of BI point out that the means test for an allowance can interact with other means tests, and with income tax and social insurance contributions, resulting in the undesirable outcome of welfare recipients having a lower net income if, for example, they return to employment from dependence on social welfare. This phenomenon is known as the 'poverty trap'. It is relevant also to persons in employment. In Ireland, for example, an employee with children may be in receipt of means-tested Family Income Supplement (FIS). An increase in pay will result in a reduction in FIS and this might combine with the loss of medical card entitlement (based on a different means test) and higher taxes and PRSI on the increased income, to result in a lower net income for the employee. This could not arise under BI, as it is paid unconditionally and is not affected by changes in gross earnings.

Fourth, BI arrangements entail the abolition of progressive tax rates and the system of tax allowances and credits. Tax allowances and credits are of less benefit to lower income taxpayers. The former confer greater cash benefits on those with higher incomes paying a higher marginal rate of tax[5]. Tax credits give the same absolute cash value to all taxpayers, but they are of no benefit to taxpayers at very low levels income, whose tax liability is less than the credits due[6]. Advocates of BI argue that the abolition of tax allowances is progressive in that they disproportionately benefit higher income taxpayers: this gain in progressivity offsets the loss arising from the abolition of higher tax rates and the implementation of one single rate of tax. The compression of tax rates, it is argued, also helps to eliminate disincentives and poverty traps.

Finally, it is contended, BI is a more suitable form of social security in today's labour market conditions. Many advanced economies are prone to large-scale unemployment and long-term unemployment and social insurance is inherently ill adapted to respond to these circumstances. The unemployed run out of entitlement to benefit and must apply for means-tested assistance; and unemployment funds relying on current social insurance contributions run in to deficits. Furthermore, social insurance is predicated on earmarked contributions from employers and employees. Employers' contributions are, in effect, a payroll tax and arguably a disincentive to employers to hire employees. Likewise, employee contributions add to their tax liabilities and may compound the disincentive effects of taxation, and they are levied on a narrow base – employee earnings.

These arguments offer a stylised account of the case for BI. The detail of individual proposals varies from one context to another and the various critiques of social insurance/social assistance systems emphasise different points. In Ireland, BI schemes have been the subject of analysis and debate since the late 1970s, starting with an NESC study in 1977 (NESC, 1977). The Commission on Taxation (1982) and the Commission on Social Welfare (1986) both considered and then rejected reforms along these lines. In the 1990s, CORI published a number of pamphlets setting the case for BI both in principle and in detail (Healy and Reynolds, 1994; Healy and Reynolds, 1995; Healy and Reynolds, 1997) and the idea was subjected to close empirical scrutiny in a number of papers (O'Toole, 1995; Ward, 1994; Callan, 1994). In 2002, a book was published (Clark and Healy, 2002) setting out detailed arguments for BI and the Government, having established a Working Group on the topic, published a Green Paper, *Basic Income*, along with detailed working papers evaluating the implications of BI (Department of An Taoiseach, 2002).

Concern about BI turns on two key points: the implications that BI would have for the tax rate required to give an unconditional income to the entire population, and the social, economic and employment effects of a universal benefit. Briefly, the BI proposal did not secure wide support at any point, and the relevant official reports and studies convey no indication of government approval for it. However, BI is relevant to the reform of pensions for two reasons.

First, even when the concept of BI as a *general* reform of the tax-benefit system is rejected, it still has a potential relevance in analysing and reforming parts of the social welfare system. For example, some of the studies of BI in Ireland have pointed to the relevance of BI as a model for reforming child income support. Currently, this part of the social welfare system comprises three different payments for different target groups: FIS for low-paid employees with children; Child Dependant Additions (CDAs) for families receiving social welfare; and Child Benefit for all families – untaxed and without a means test. In spite of this three-cornered provision, child poverty remains high, FIS creates disincentives and, because of its complexity, there is less than complete take-up, and CDAs may create employment disincentives among the unemployed with children. Some analyses of child income support have pointed to the potential of a Basic Income for Children (BIC) as a solution to these problems. By analogy, BIC would entail the payment of one adequate payment for all children, simplifying the system and dealing with the incentives problems.

For opponents of BI, one of its least acceptable features is the unconditional nature of the benefit – it would be paid, whether or not it was needed and at the possible cost of a widespread disincentive to work. But in the case of children and the elderly, employment incentives are *not* a central policy consideration. It might be argued, in fact, that BI for older persons – a universal payment without a means test, contribution requirements or retirement conditions – would be highly appropriate: it would offer a basis on which beneficiaries could build their 'income package', allowing them to supplement their incomes with earnings, income from savings, pension income, and so on.

The second reason why BI is relevant to old age pensions is that much of the reasoning leading to support for BI applies to pensioners and pension issues. A BI arrangement would offer a simple, gender-neutral payment, not conditional on retirement. It could resolve the complications arising from the means test, rules about dependency, and the retirement condition attaching to the RP.

But is such an approach feasible in the Irish context and what, in practice, would it entail? It is important to note that this chapter is *not* advocating the outright implementation of BI as a substitute for the current suite of State pensions, but simply outlining how the current system might be developed in a way that draws on the strengths of BI. The objective here is to outline a general model without offering details or estimates of the costs and numbers affected. A strategy along these lines might comprise the following elements:

- A 'Basic Pension' for all citizens above a certain age, untaxed and without a means test, and the abolition of the age tax credit;
- A second–tier State pension, related strictly to social insurance contributions, without redistributive elements such as credits;

- A continuation of the regulatory regime for occupational pensions and PRSAs;

- A significant curtailment of the tax incentives for occupational pensions, PRSAs and Approved Retirement Funds; and

- Integration of occupational pensions with the Basic Pension.

This design recognises the fact that a pensions system, of necessity, must incorporate a number of competing values, that reform must build to some extent on existing provisions and expectations, and command broad public and political support. Arguably, the approach suggested here, in its totality, would achieve a number of objectives.

By having a universal pension funded out of general taxation, the system would have a distinctly redistributive dimension. It would also ensure independent pensions for all men and women. This Basic Pension could also incorporate the Living Alone supplement and the Age supplement for those aged 80+ that are integral to the current system. However, the approach set out here also envisages the retention of a social insurance tier. The history of pensions provision shows that there is strong social and political attachment to the underlying principle of social insurance: that those in employment generate the revenue to pay the current costs of pensions, unemployment benefit and other benefits. There is also a universal acceptance that the form of rights generated by social insurance are preferable to the complexities and indignities of means tested benefits- although social insurance entitlements are *not* actuarially related to the details of individuals' financial contributions. In the framework proposed here, the second tier social insurance pension would not have dependants' additions; the pension could simply be an additional pension, with the amounts tiered in the same manner as the current pensions, *or* it could be designed on an income-related basis. The important feature of this proposal is that it would relate pensions only to (earned) contributions thereby strengthening its role as a benefit clearly based on past participation in the economy. At present, flat-rate social insurance pensions attempt to conflate a series of roles- poverty relief, support for dependants of pensioners, recognition of 'unearned' contributions, redistribution, and income replacement: this has the effect of diluting the social insurance nature of the system and introducing quite complex and perhaps unintended redistribution of contributions and benefits. A combination of a Basic Pension and a contribution-related pension allows a series of objectives to be pursued using two tiers of the pension system rather than one.

Further elements in the proposed strategy are the retention and improvement of the regulatory regime for occupational pensions and PRSAs (see Chapter 4) and the substantial reduction in tax allowances for such pensions. The case for the latter arises from the data in Chapter 6 showing the substantial cost of the tax-treatment of these pensions and their very regressive distribution. In the proposal here, a significant saving on the tax allowances would go a substantial distance towards the funding of a Basic Pension. Clearly such a policy change could not be implemented overnight.

A final element in the proposal is to retain, as at present, a method of integrating State pensions and occupational pensions. If a Basic Pension were introduced in the context of a second tier, contribution-based social insurance pension, it would then be appropriate to use the Basic one in the integration formula.

It is important to stress that these proposals are not as dramatic as might seem at first sight. Existing State pensions already encompass a substantial section of the older population: a Basic Pension effectively gives 100 per cent cover. Also, the social insurance pension system – on both the benefit and contribution sides – is well established and over time it will become substantially more comprehensive as future cohorts of public sector employees acquire social insurance rights. As regards the reduction or elimination of tax deductions, the equity case was referred to earlier. Equally important is the fact that the tax deductions have not led to a growth in occupational pensions coverage, and it is not clear that the PRSAs will make up for this large deficiency.

One important point about any Basic Income or Basic Pension idea is the absence of a means test and/or its exclusion from taxation: there is by no means universal acceptance of wholly non-targeted benefits. This raises a number of issues, but clearly it would be possible to have some element of targeting while still conforming to the core principle of BI. For example, the Basic Pension could be defined as taxable income, but the pension and tax systems could be co-ordinated so that the level of tax credits would result in pensioners not having a tax liability where the Basic Pension was their only income. Alternatively, a limited form of means testing could be applied to the Basic Pension, one that would exclude only those on the very highest incomes rather than including only those on the very lowest. 'Capped universalism' is the term used to describe this kind of means testing which has been a feature of social policy in Australia and New Zealand.

5.5 IMPLEMENTING POLICY REFORM

What would be the route to the kind of policy being proposed here? The key to implementing the reform would be to first develop the State pension on a phased basis so that it systematically takes on more of the attributes of a Basic Pension. This would mean a cumulative easing of the means test, combined with the individualisation of pensions i.e. the means test to be based on personal rather than marital income, and dependants (of pensionable age) of contributory pensioners, to be awarded a pension directly in their own right.

A second element of reform, not necessarily sequential, would be the transformation of the OACP and RP into a second–tier pension, based wholly on contributions. This would essentially entail 're-packaging' the income of pensioners so that existing insurance pensioners received the Basic Pension and the new social insurance pension. The latter would be adjusted so that it would conform to a more strictly contribution-based regime. Individual pensioners entitled to an insurance pension would receive one pension, but based on the separate components of the Basic and Insurance pensions. This change would leave the existing administration of social insurance contributions and payments intact, but the amount of pension payable under the new scheme would depend on the contribution history of the pensioner, with 'contribution' in this context referring almost exclusively to paid contributions.

A third component of the reform is the reduction of the tax subsidies to occupational and private pensions. These could not be abolished or substantially reduced overnight. A starting point for reform might be the option discussed in the final report of the National Pensions Board – to place a 'cap' on the amount of tax deductibility for individual tax-payers and over time to significantly reduce the level of deductibility. The tax treatment of occupational pensions is an 'EET' regime: contributions are tax exempt (E), investment income and capital gains on pension funds are also exempt (E), while the pension income received by the pensioner is counted as taxable income (T). Pension systems in other countries vary in the kind of tax regime that applies to occupational schemes. The significant point is that Ireland's (EET) regime can be reformed so that the tax base can be considerably widened, and a Basic Pension funded in part by the revenue raised.

Undoubtedly, pension reform requires a long-term perspective and policy makers need to phase in changes over time and offer some clarity to prospective pensioners about the pension regime they will face. One added argument for the system proposed here is that the population would acquire certainty about one element in the pension system.

It is also important to note that while no government has introduced a Basic Income system some countries have had for a long time the kind of Basic Pension advocated here, or implemented provisions that reflect BI principles – universality, pensions based on individual rights, and so on. Finland, for example, has a national guaranteed pension, without a means test, based on residence: this puts a floor under the income replacement social insurance pension. An element of targeting is incorporated by withdrawing the national pension if the level of the social insurance pension exceeds a threshold.

New Zealand offers a well-documented example of a country that has adapted Basic Income-type ideas to its pensions requirements (St. John, 1992; St. John, 1999; St. John and Gran, 2003). Two New Zealand authorities summarised its pension system in these terms (St John and Gran, 2003, p.200):

> In 2000, the NZ system for retirement income remained unique in the OECD. It was remarkably simple, based on the provision of a non-contributory, flat-rate pension for individuals who qualified by virtue of age and residency, and voluntary savings. Thus there were no compulsory savings schemes and no tax incentives for private saving for retirement.
>
> Eligibility for the State pension, now called New Zealand Superannuation, is based on meeting the qualifying age (65 by 2001) and simple residency require-ments, ten years since age 20 and five years since age 50.

Briefly, the principle of a universal unconditional pension has a long history of support there. In 1938, New Zealand's Social Security Act established an Age Benefit (means-tested and subject to a test of character) and Universal Superannuation, a flat–rate benefit for all aged over 65. These two pensions were co-ordinated so that at age 65 those in receipt of the Age Benefit could continue to receive it or opt to take the taxable Universal Superannuation. This system remained in place (with both benefits increasing significantly in real terms) until the mid-1970s.

In 1974, the New Zealand Superannuation Act was passed, introducing a form of national insurance. The reason for this was the low coverage of occupational schemes and hence the absence of any income replacement element in the pensions of most retired persons. The new pension was to be based on the employers' and employees' contributions, with pensioners receiving annuities purchased from their individual accounts at age 65. Under this scheme pensions were to be purely actuarial. This departure from a simple universal benefit did not take root – the scheme was abandoned after one year and the contributions returned. In the policy controversy that triggered the demise of the new arrangements, a number of grounds of disquiet were expressed: fear of the State's control and regulation of the accumulating investment funds; disquiet at the likely inferior, actuarially-calculated pensions women would receive; the absence of any redistributive dimension; and, inadequate provision for survivors' pensions. However, the critical factor in the failure to introduce this insurance pension was the promise by the political opposition of a simpler, more generous pension that would be particularly attractive to women.

In 1977, the New Zealand government abolished the Age Benefit and the Universal Superannuation and established in their place the National Superannuation (NS) system. NS was a Pay–As-You-Go pension, funded from general taxation, set at 80 per cent of gross average wage for married couples and 48 per cent for single pensioners. It was an individual, taxable pension payable at age 60, subject to residential requirements. Many of the features of NS, including the individual basis of the pension whereby a married person received one half of the gross married rate, taxed in his or her own name, were praised as 'good for women' (St. John and Gran, 2003, p. 204). NS was not means-tested and not subject to a retirement condition, but the trend towards rising marginal tax rates in a progressive tax rate structure ensured that by the early 1980s the net benefit of NS was lower for high income pensioners. On the introduction of NS, (St. John and Gran, 2003, p. 205) state:

> The retired immediately benefited, and problems of poverty among the aged virtually disappeared. One of the significant features was the generosity, not only to

women and those who had not been in the labour force, but to those aged 60 and older who had not yet retired, as there was no earnings test. When it was implemented, NS probably provided the most generous State pension in the world. It was not limited to previous paid labour force participants, but available to every older resident, simple to understand and people could easily predict the pension they would receive.

Subsequently, during a period of retrenchment in the public finances, NS was modified. In 1984, a 'surcharge' (effectively a means test) of 25 per cent on retirees' other income was implemented; this was later reduced to 18 per cent, and later again increased to 20 per cent. During the 1980s and 1990s, pensions policy – and in particular the question of targeting – was a constant source of controversy, resulting in an attempt to reach an all–party accord on pension provision. The net outcome was that the pension age was increased, the targeting measures were in place until 1997 and were finally abolished in 1998. Significantly – and in contrast to Ireland – tax neutrality for saving for retirement was implemented. During the 1990s, the level of the NS fell relative to earnings, resulting in a rise in poverty (measured on a relative income basis). Labour force participation among older men and women began to rise again in the late 1990s in response to the declining relative value of NS and the increased age of entitlement.

None of this is to suggest that Ireland should attempt to imitate the detail of New Zealand's or any country's policies. What this account has shown is that it is possible to construct a pension regime that gives considerable weight to simplicity, gender equality and poverty reduction if policy focuses on strengthening the State's pension provision. An integral part of this strategy is to avoid the complexity, cost and inequity of tax-based instruments designed to increase private savings and sustain occupational pensions. Direct pensions paid to all, with minimal targeting, are a better use of public revenues.

5.6 CONCLUSION

Ireland's pension system has undergone significant change, but fundamentally the State's role in pensions has exhibited remarkable continuity. It is still developing within the long-established Beveridge model of social security – social insurance complemented by social assistance. This chapter has argued that State pensions should in future develop along more universal lines, and that the model for State pensions should resemble that of a Basic Pension. The state should offer a pension based on citizenship (or residence), without means tests or contribution requirements, while retaining social insurance and converting this to a second–tier, possibly income-related pension. This would result in a simpler, fairer pension system if the costly, inequitable tax supports for private and occupational pensions were significantly reduced or abolished.

Public and political debate about social security in Ireland is bedevilled by a focus on the level of benefits and on their annual, marginal adjustment. It is equally necessary – especially in the area of pensions – to begin to debate the future structure of pensions provisions.

The next chapter gives detailed evidence on the size and distribution of the subsidy granted via tax reliefs to funded occupational pension schemes, and hence the potential for diverting resources into a universal Basic Pension.

Notes

1   Those reaching age 66 on or after 2012 will require at least 520 (full-rate) contributions, regardless of the yearly average.
2   These details are also relevant. The bar on employment for RP recipients is not absolute. They can work part-time (in non-insurable employment)

and earn up to a certain amount, or engage in self-employment up to a certain level of income. The tiered level of payments for RP varies between the maximum payment and minimum payment, based on average yearly contributions of 48 and 24, respectively.
3 The procedure is that the first €13,000 is disregarded in calculating means. Above that threshold, a weekly income is imputed in ascending bands: for example, an applicant with €25,000 savings will have approximately the first €12,500 disregarded, and the next €12,500 will be counted as the equivalent of €1.27 income per week. Income estimated in this way would offset any NCOAP entitlement.
4 The relevant section of the official website giving information to the public about entitlement to the contributory pension comprises 15 pages. These pages do not give details about benefit levels – a further section of the site contains this information.
5. For example, a taxpayer paying the current higher marginal tax rate of 42 per cent would get the cash equivalent value of €420 from a tax allowance of €1,000 (€1,000 @ 42 per cent), while a taxpayer on a marginal rate of 20 per cent would get the equivalent of €200 (€1,000 @ 20 per cent).
6. This is a simplification, of course. Tax credits can be made refundable, so that a low income person whose tax liability is less than the credits can have the difference refunded, thereby structuring the tax system so that it is, in effect, paying a benefit to in the form a 'negative tax'.

References

Beveridge, Sir William (1942), *Social Insurance and Allied Services*, London: H.M.S.O.

Callan, T., C. O'Donoghue and C. O'Neil (1994), *Analysis of a Basic Income Scheme for Ireland*, Dublin: Economic and Social Research Institute, Policy Research Series paper no. 21.

Central Statistics Office (2005), *Survey of Income and Living Conditions*, Dublin: Central Statistics Office.

Clark, C. and S. Healy (2002), *Basic Income Guarantee*, Dublin: The Liffey Press.

Commission on Taxation (1982), *First Report of the Commission on Taxation: Direct Taxation*, Dublin: Stationery Office (Pl. 617).

Department of Social Welfare (1976), *A National Income

Related Pension Scheme, Dublin: Stationery Office.

Department of Social Welfare (1978), *Social Insurance for the Self-Employed*, Dublin: Stationery Office.

Department of An Taoiseach, Green Paper (2002), *A Basic Income*, Dublin: Stationery Office.

Healy, S. and B. Reynolds (1994), *Towards an Adequate Income Guarantee*, Dublin: Conference of Religious of Ireland.

Healy, S. and B. Reynolds (1995), *An Adequate Income Guarantee for All*, Dublin: Conference of Religious of Ireland.

Healy, S. and B. Reynolds (1997), *Surfing the Income Net*, Dublin: Conference of Religious of Ireland.

McCashin, A. (2004), *Social Security in Ireland*, Dublin: Gill and Macmillan.

Minister for Social Welfare, (1985) *Address by the Minister at First Annual Conference of the Retirement Planning Council of Ireland*, Dublin.

Murphy, M. (2003), *Valuing Care Work*, Dublin: National Women's Council.

National Pensions Board (1987), *First Report*, Dublin: Government Publications.

National Pensions Board (1988), *Report on the Extension of Social Insurance to the Self-Employed*, Dublin: Government Publications.

National Pensions Board (1993), *Developing the National Pension System*, Dublin: Government Publications.

NESC (1978), *Integrated Approaches to Taxes and Transfers*, Report No. 37, Dublin: Stationery Office.

O Grada, C. (2002), *"'The Greatest Blessing of All': The Old Age Pension in Ireland"*, Oxford: The Past and Present Society (Oxford).

O'Toole, F. (1995), "The Costings of a Basic Income Scheme" in Healy, S. and B. Reynolds (eds.) *Towards an Adequate Income Guarantee*, Dublin: Conference of Religious of Ireland.

Pensions Board (1998), *Securing Retirement Income*, Dublin:

Pensions Board.

St. John, A. (1992), "National Superannuation: Or How Not to Make Policy" in, Boston, J. and P. Dalziel (eds.) *The Decent Society. Essays in Response to National's Economic and Social Policies,* Oxford: Oxford University Press.

St. John, A. (1999), "Superannuation in the 1990s: Where Angels Fear to Tread?" in Boston, J., P. Dalziel and S. St. John (eds.) *Redesigning the Welfare State. Problems, Prospects, Policies,* Auckland: Oxford University Press.

St. John, A. and B. Gran (2003), "The World's Social Laboratory: Women-friendly Aspects of New Zealand Pensions" in Ginn, J., D. Street and S. Arber (eds.) *Women, Work and Pensions: International Issues and Prospects,* Buckingham: Open University Press.

Ward, S. (1994), "A Basic Income System for Ireland" in Healy, S. and B. Reynolds (eds.) *Towards An Adequate Income For All,* Dublin: Conference of Religious of Ireland.

Whelan, C. T., R. Layte, B. Maitre, B. Gannon, B. Nolan, D. Watson, and J. Williams (2003), *Monitoring Poverty Trends in Ireland: Results from the 2001 Living in Ireland Survey,* Dublin: Economic and Social Research Institute, Policy Research Series, no. 51.

Chapter 6

Pension Tax Reliefs and Equity[1]

BY GERARD HUGHES

6.1. INTRODUCTION

Many of those who argue for the use of tax incentives to encourage the expansion of the private pension system do so in the belief that private provision is less costly to the Exchequer than public provision and that the favourable tax arrangements for the private pension system are broadly equitable[2]. For example, the representative body of the pensions industry, the Irish Association of Pension Funds (1998, p. 1) has argued that "it is a common misconception that pension funds are exempt from tax" because "they actually operate on the basis of deferred taxation NOT no taxation" and that "the exemptions are balanced by the eventual taxation of benefits (except, of course, in relation to the lump sum) so the net effect is a tax deferral rather than an outright exemption" (Irish Association of Pension Funds, 1999, p. 1). Despite these claims that the Government ultimately gets back most of the tax forgone on pension contributions and pension fund investment income by taxing pension benefits, it is striking that the pensions industry uses the favourable tax treatment of private pensions as a major selling point for its products.

The Pensions Board, the government's advisory body

on pensions, appears to share the views of the pensions industry on the tax arrangements for private pensions. It argued in its report on developing the national pension system (Pensions Board, 1998 p. 146) that "the tax treatment of pensions, other than lump sums, is essentially tax deferral". Its predecessor, the National Pensions Board, also took a favourable view of the tax arrangements for private pensions. It argued (National Pensions Board, 1988) that "the present tax treatment of pension funds is simple to understand and operate, is broadly equitable and clearly acts as a major encouragement to the establishment of funded occupational pension schemes".

These arguments will be considered in this paper. Section 6.2 examines how the aggregate cost of tax incentives for the private pension system has grown over the last two decades or so. Section 6.3 compares the cost of tax reliefs for the private pension system with the cost of direct expenditure on the public pension system. Section 6.4 considers how the coverage of the private pension system has changed over time. Section 6.5 presents information on how the tax reliefs on pension contributions by employees to occupational pension schemes and by the self-employed to Retirement Annuity Contracts are distributed by income group. Section 6.6 contains a summary and conclusions.

6.2. ESTIMATES OF THE COST OF TAX RELIEFS ON OCCUPATIONAL PENSIONS

The income tax reliefs on employee and employer pension contributions and pension fund investments and other items of expenditure, such as contributions to voluntary health insurance and mortgage repayments, amount in effect to expenditure programmes delivered through the tax system. The term "tax expenditure" is used to bring out the similarity between government support for private pensions and government expenditure on public pension schemes. For example, the Commission on Taxation (1982, p. 87) argued that tax expenditures "are equivalent in terms of revenue foregone to direct Government expenditure and should in general be judged by the same criteria and subjected to the same review process."

Occupational pension schemes in Ireland receive favourable tax treatment by applying to the Revenue Commissioners for "exempt approved status". To qualify for this special status, a scheme must be established under an irrevocable trust, the assets of the fund must be held apart from the employer's other assets, and disposed of in accordance with a deed of trust. As none of the Government agencies responsible for the operation of private occupational pension schemes publish statistics on the financial operations of these schemes, the Revenue Commissioners have had to base their estimates of the cost of tax reliefs for occupational pensions on limited information that can be gleaned from different sources. Their estimates of the cost of tax reliefs for Retirement Annuity Contracts are derived from information on pension contributions in the annual tax returns of the self-employed. Since 1980/81, the Revenue Commissioners have published annual estimates of the cost to the Exchequer of the tax support for occupational pension schemes and of Retirement Annuity Contracts for the self-employed. Their most comprehensive annual estimate for occupational pension schemes is based on total contributions by employers and employees, plus the investment income of the pension funds minus the amount paid out in pension benefits and lump sums. The Revenue Commissioners estimates show that the combined cost of the tax reliefs for occupational pension schemes and personal pensions for the self-employed is now the largest item in the annual list of tax allowances and tax reliefs[3].

Figure 6.1 shows the Revenue Commissioners estimates of the cost of pension tax reliefs on the net income of occupational pension funds and on pension schemes for the self-employed for the tax years from 1980/81 to 2000/01. Over the whole period the cost of tax reliefs for occupational pension schemes rose from €38 million to €1,292 million. The cost of the tax relief on pension contributions made by the self-employed rose from €13 million to €205 million. In total, the cost of tax reliefs on pension contributions for employees and the self-employed increased from €51 million in 1980/81 to €1,497 million in 2000/01.

Fig. 6.1 Cost of Tax Expenditures on Private Pensions for Employees and Self-Employed, 1980/81 – 2000/01

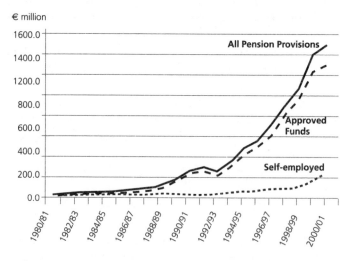

Relative to GNP, as Figure 6.2 shows, the real cost of pension tax relief for employees more than quadrupled from about one-third of a percentage point in 1980/81 to 1.5 per cent in 2000/01. For the self-employed, the cost more than doubled from 0.1 per cent of GNP in 1980/81 to 0.2 per cent in 2000/01. In total, the resource cost of tax reliefs for private pension arrangements quadrupled from 0.4 per cent of GNP in 1980/81 to 1.7 per cent in 2000/01.

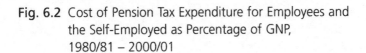

Fig. 6.2 Cost of Pension Tax Expenditure for Employees and the Self-Employed as Percentage of GNP, 1980/81 – 2000/01

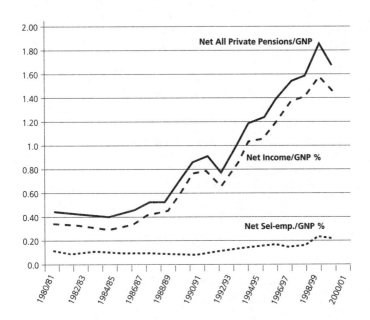

6.3. TAX EXPENDITURE ON PRIVATE AND DIRECT EXPENDITURE ON PUBLIC PENSIONS

At the end of the 1980s, it was realised that ageing of the population in the early decades of the 21st century would increase the cost of State pension schemes in many OECD countries. Governments began to look for ways of changing the balance between public and private pension provision in an attempt to avoid raising taxes in the future (see OECD 1992). As well as the problem of population ageing, Ireland faced additional problems as the flat-rate public pension benefits were too low to adequately replace income from work for most workers, who did not have a State earnings-related pension scheme, and the coverage of occupational pension schemes was low and very unevenly distributed across sectors and occupations (see Figures 6.3 and 6.4, derived from the ESRI Living in Ireland Survey, 2000).

Fig. 6.3 Percentage of Employees with Pension Entitlements by Occupation, 2000

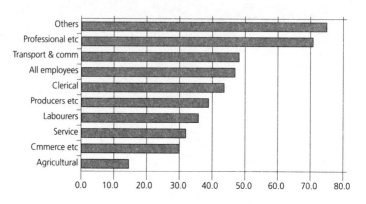

Fig. 6.4 Percentage of Employees with Pension Entitlement by Sector, 2000

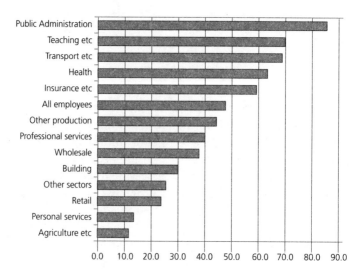

The strategy recommended by the Pensions Board (1998) to cope with these problems is to gradually raise the flat-rate State pension up to 34 per cent of average industrial earnings, to accumulate a National Pension Reserve Fund for investment in financial assets selected from global financial markets, and to try to increase pension coverage on a voluntary basis by providing access to Personal Retirement Savings Accounts (PRSAs)[4]. The Pensions Board (1998, p. 109) noted that "the purpose of the fund would be to place a ceiling on the additional Exchequer contribution required for [social welfare pensions for] the foreseeable future". It recommended that Personal Retirement Savings Accounts should receive the same favourable tax treatment as occupational pension schemes. It did not provide any comparisons of past trends in Exchequer expenditure on social welfare pensions relative to tax expenditure on private pensions nor did it include in its projections out to 2046 estimates of tax expenditure on existing private pensions or on the Personal Retirement Savings Accounts which it proposed should be introduced to increase private pension coverage on a voluntary basis. Although the Board's strategy relies heavily on generous pension tax incentives, it did not consider how effective existing tax reliefs for private pensions have been in promoting coverage or how effective private pension schemes are in actually providing income during retirement.

The policy message which comes through the various reports published as part of the National Pensions Policy Initiative is that public pension schemes should be restricted to paying modest flat-rate benefits while earnings-related pension benefits should be provided on a voluntary basis by private financial institutions on the assumption that private provision will be less costly to the Exchequer (see Pensions Board, 1997 and 1998). In order to assess the argument that private provision is less costly, the trend in the cost of tax expenditure on occupational and personal pensions will be compared with the trend in the cost of direct expenditure on the State's old age pension schemes. Then the trend in the coverage of occupational pensions will be examined to see how effective the provision of tax incentives for private pensions has been in promoting pension coverage.

There are three social welfare pension schemes that have to be considered: the Retirement Pension Scheme, the Old Age (Contributory) Pension Scheme, and the means-tested Old Age (Non-Contributory) Pension Scheme. The main difference between the two contributory schemes is that the retirement pension is payable at age 65 provided the person is retired from insurable employment and satisfies the social insurance contribution conditions, whereas the contributory old age pension is payable at age 66 to those who satisfy the contribution conditions. Applicants for a non-contributory pension have to satisfy a means test to be eligible for a flat-rate social assistance pension. The contributory old age pension scheme is financed on a pay-as-you-go basis by Pay-Related Social Insurance (PRSI) contributions by employers, employees and the self-employed, while the retirement pension scheme is financed by similar contributions by employers and employees. Any shortfall between income and expenditure on the two contributory public pension schemes is met by the State out of general taxation. The non-contributory old age pension scheme is also paid for out of general taxation.

Tax expenditure on occupational pensions and direct expenditure on social welfare pensions are compared in Figure 6.5 for the period 1980/81-2000/01. At the beginning of the period in 1980/81, tax expenditure on private pensions amounted to just over a quarter of direct expenditure on the contributory social insurance pension schemes, €51 million versus €194 million. By the end of the period, it had increased to 128 per cent of expenditure on the contributory schemes, €1,497 million versus €1,172 million. With respect to the non-contributory social assistance pension scheme, tax expenditure on private pensions increased from 28 per cent in 1980/81, €51 million versus €178 million, to 328 per cent in 2000/01, €1,497 million versus €456 million.

Fig. 6.5 Direct Expenditure on Contributory and Non-Contributory Public Pensions and Tax Expenditure on Occupational and Self-Employed Private Pensions, 1980/81-2000/01

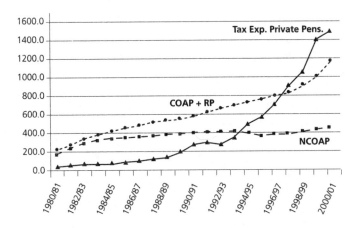

In terms of the combined social welfare pension schemes, the cost of tax expenditure on private pension schemes increased from 13 per cent in 1980, €51 million versus €372 million, to 92 per cent by 2000/01, €1,497million versus €1,628 million. Thus the cost of tax reliefs for private pensions now exceeds the cost of direct expenditure on the contributory and non-contributory public pension schemes considered separately. Taking the two public pension schemes together, the cost of the tax reliefs for private schemes is only 8 per cent less than the combined cost of direct expenditure on public pension schemes. The introduction in 2003 of Personal Retirement Savings

Accounts (PRSAs), which also receive favourable tax treatment to encourage individuals to save for their pension, is likely to further increase the cost of the tax reliefs for private pensions. If the cost of the tax expenditure on private pensions continues to grow as it has in the recent past it will not be long before it exceeds the cost of direct expenditure on both the contributory and means-tested public pension schemes.

It is evident from the trends in tax expenditure on private pensions and direct expenditure on public pensions that the cost of the tax forgone to subsidise private pensions was less costly than expenditure on public pension schemes at the beginning of the period under review. However, this is no longer the case. Now the cost of the tax forgone on private pensions is almost as great as the combined cost of direct expenditure on the contributory and non-contributory State pension schemes.

6.4. TRENDS IN COVERAGE OF OCCUPATIONAL PENSION SCHEMES

One of the long-term objectives of the favourable tax arrangements for private pensions is to increase their coverage. What progress has been made towards this objective? There is very little statistical information available on trends in the coverage of private pension schemes for the self-employed, so this question cannot be answered with any certainty in relation to this group. However, there is sufficient data available from a Department of Social Welfare (Ireland, 1976) report for 1975, an ESRI survey by Keogh and Whelan (1985) for 1985 and annual data from the Pensions Board for 1992 and subsequent years to allow this question to be answered for occupational pension schemes for employees.

The percentage of those at work covered by occupational pension schemes over the period 1975-2003 is shown in

Figure 6.6. This figure also shows what percentage of people at work belonged to occupational pension schemes for employees in the private and public sectors of the economy in the period for which data is available from the Pensions Board Annual Report from 1992 onwards. Coverage data for the self-employed is not shown in this figure as information for it is only available from special surveys carried out as part of the Quarterly National Household Survey in the second quarter of 2002 and the first quarter of 2004. Figure 6.6 shows that in 1975 only a minority of those at work, 35 per cent, were members of occupational pension schemes. Pension coverage for employees increased by 9 percentage points between 1975 and 1985 to 44 per cent. However, coverage fell after that by 8 percentage points to 36 per cent in 1998. Thereafter, there was a recovery in coverage that brought the figure up to 41 per cent. However, the recovery has not been strong enough to bring the coverage figure back to the level it was at in 1985.

Fig. 6.6 Public and Private Sector Occupational Pension Plan Coverage Rates 1975-2003

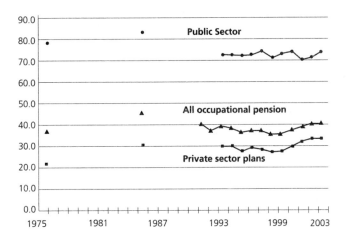

The main effect of the favourable tax arrangements for occupational pension schemes should have been experienced by private pension plans which are covered by the funding standard set by the Pensions Act 1990. Membership of such schemes is predominantly concentrated in the private sector. Most public sector occupational plans are not covered by the funding standard as they are either financed on a pay-as-you-go basis, or even though funded, have been granted an exemption where the State remains liable for some benefits (see section 52 of Pensions Act, 1990). Consequently, their development has been largely unaffected by the existence of favourable tax arrangements for occupational pension plans. In order to examine if there has been any increase in coverage rates that could be attributed to pension tax reliefs, Figure 6 shows the coverage rates for private and public sector plans.

The coverage rates for both public and private sector occupational pension plans increased significantly between 1975 and 1985. Coverage in the public sector increased by about 4 percentage points while in the private sector it rose by over 8 percentage points. Relatively, the increase in the private sector coverage over this period was much greater than the increase in the public sector and the tax reliefs for occupational plans may have contributed to this growth. After 1985, however, the coverage rate in both sectors fell to a low of 71 per cent in the public sector and 27 per cent in the private sector in 1998. Coverage in both sectors has recovered since then to reach 74 per cent in the public sector and 33 per cent in the private sector. Overall the occupational pension coverage rate in the private sector has been fairly stable over the last two decades and there is no evidence that the tax incentives have had a noticeable effect on private sector coverage during this period.

The data shows, therefore, that there has been modest growth in pension coverage but that all of this growth occurred in the ten years 1975-85. During the period since then, pension coverage fell to a low of about 36 per cent in

1998 and then recovered to reach 41 per cent in 2003. Despite the continuing substantial support provided through the tax system for occupational pension schemes, they are providing coverage for only one-third of those working in the private sector and there is little evidence of long-term growth in their coverage.

An important consequence of the low level of coverage of the private pension system is that despite the financial support provided for it, the great majority of pensioners are dependent on the public pension system for most of their income during retirement, as Jim Stewart has shown in Chapter 2 using data from the Household Budget Survey. The outcome, using the ESRI Living in Ireland Survey data for pensioner couples and single pensioners, is similar. Table 6.1 shows that 91 per cent of all pensioner units received a social welfare pension in 2000 and that the amount they received provided 56 per cent of their retirement income. Only a third of all pensioner units received an income from private pension schemes and these schemes provided less than a quarter of average retirement income.

Table 6.1:   Percentage of All Pensioner Units Having Income from Various Sources in 2000

Source of Income	Ireland	
	Per cent with Income from this Source	Per cent of Total Income
Social welfare (public) pension	91	56
Occupational/personal (private) pension	33	23
Investment income	27	7
Earnings	11	14
Other income	1	0
Total	100	100

Sources: Hughes and Watson (2005).
Note: A pensioner unit is defined as a single (non-cohabiting) person aged 65 years and over or a couple (married or cohabiting) where the man is aged 65 and over. Income may derive from a number of different sources.

6.5. WHO BENEFITS FROM TAX RELIEFS ON PRIVATE PENSIONS?

Because tax reliefs on occupational pension contributions by employees are given before income tax and PRSI are deducted, the Revenue Commissioners do not have any data on the distribution of tax reliefs for occupational pension schemes. However, they do have data on the distribution of tax reliefs on Retirement Annuity Contracts from the annual tax returns made by the self-employed. Fortunately, the ESRI Living in Ireland Surveys for 1998 and 2000 (see Nolan, Gannon, Layte, Watson, Whelan and Williams, 2002) collected information on membership of occupational pension schemes and employee pension contributions. This information is used in this section to examine who benefits from the tax reliefs on private pension schemes.

Table 6.2: Employees and Self-Employed Ranked by Weekly Gross Earnings Showing the Percentage with Occupational Pension Entitlements or Retirement Annuity Contracts by Income Deciles

Decile	Employees 2000	Self-Employed 1999/00
First	4.1	3.4
Second	6.3	9.7
Third	20.3	20.2
Fourth	29.8	34.9
Fifth	32.4	48.9
Sixth	43.0	55.6
Seventh	59.5	62.5
Eighth	68.5	71.5
Ninth	79.4	70.9
Tenth	81.1	60.2

Source: ESRI Living in Ireland Survey 2000 and Revenue Commissioners special tabulations.
Note the income deciles are approximate and they are estimated separately for employees and the self-employed.

Table 6.2 and Figure 6.7 show the percentage in each income decile of employees in 2000 and self-employed in 1999/00 that were covered by an occupational or personal pension scheme. The table shows that the coverage of occupational pension schemes and personal pension schemes for the self-employed is quite high for the top three deciles, moderate for those in the fifth, sixth and seventh deciles, poor for those in the third and fourth deciles, and very poor for the two bottom income deciles[5]. Coverage rates for both employees and the self-employed increase steadily from very low levels in the bottom income deciles (3 per cent to 10 per cent) to quite high levels in the top income deciles (60 per cent to 80 per cent).

This pattern of pension coverage is very striking. Hughes and Nolan (1999) argue that differences in coverage rates for employees can be understood in terms of a segmented labour market model in which pension benefits are offered by employers as part of the total compensation package for moderate to high paying jobs to attract and hold onto well qualified employees. They argue that pension benefits are not part of the compensation package for low paying jobs as there is generally an excess supply of applicants for these jobs and high turnover rates.

As already noted, the ESRI Living in Ireland Survey data contains information on the size of the employee contribution to occupational pension schemes but unfortunately not on the employer contribution. An estimate of the value of the tax relief on employee contributions to occupational pension schemes was made by Maitre and Nolan (2001) using data from the 1998 survey. Their data and the Revenue Commissioners data on pensions tax relief for the self-employed in 1999/00 are used in Figure 6.8 to compare the distribution of pension tax reliefs by income quintile for employees and the self employed[6]. The pattern for the two groups is similar. Almost two-thirds of the tax relief for employees goes to the highest paid employees in the top quintile and only 1 per cent goes to the lowest paid employees in the bottom quintile.

Figure 6.7 Pension Coverage of Employees and Self-Employed by Income Decile Around 2000

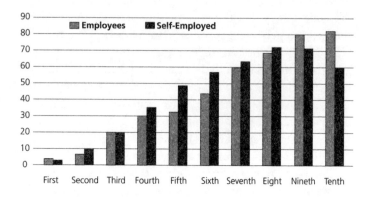

Figure 6.8 Distribution by Income Quintile of Pension Tax Reliefs on Employees' Contributions and Self-Employed Contributions Around 2000

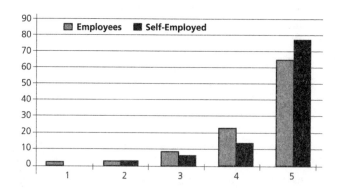

Over three-quarters of the tax relief on pension contributions by the self-employed goes to the highest earners in the top quintile and less than half a per cent goes to the lowest earners in the bottom quintile. The distribution of the tax reliefs among the self-employed is even more concentrated than in the case of employees. Over three-quarters of all the tax relief accrues to self-employed people in the top quintile while virtually none of it accrues to those in the bottom quintile.

The concentration of tax reliefs for private pensions on those in the highest income groups is similar to the outcomes found by Hughes and Sinfield (2004) for the United Kingdom and the United States which have similar tax arrangements to Ireland's in order to encourage the growth of private pension schemes. The concentration of pension tax reliefs on the highest income groups in Ireland is an example of the 'upside-down' or regressive nature of tax expenditures whereby, as Sinfield (1997, p. 20) notes:

> The benefit is greater, the higher the income and the higher the marginal tax rate which is avoided as a result of the tax mechanism. The greatest beneficiaries are those who have the least needs by any measure used in social policy analysis.

There are two main reasons for this regressive outcome, as Agulnik and Le Grand (1998) point out. The first is that membership of occupational pension schemes and contributions to Retirement Annuity Contracts increase strongly with income as we have seen. The second is that the tax relief is given at the highest marginal rate of tax. Hence, the value of the tax relief as a percentage of income rises as income rises. The interaction of these two factors results in a steady increase in the absolute value of the tax relief on pension contributions as the absolute value of income rises.

6.6. SUMMARY AND CONCLUSIONS

The evidence presented in this paper shows that the annual cost to the Exchequer of tax relief on pensions is substantial. It has grown from €51 million in 1980/81 to €1.4 billion in 2000/01 or from 0.4 per cent to 1.7 per cent of

GDP. Over the same period, the cost of the public social insurance pension system has grown from €194 million to €1,172 million. Hence, the argument that the private pension system is less costly than the public system is not supported by the evidence.

The trend in relation to the coverage of occupational pension schemes suggests that tax incentives for pension saving have failed to provide pension coverage for the majority of workers and that pension coverage of occupational pension schemes has been fairly stable since 1985. Consequently, the evidence does not support the argument that providing tax incentives for pension saving will gradually extend pension coverage to a majority of the working population.

The present tax treatment of the private pension system is inequitable. Most of the tax reliefs accrue to the highest paid employees or the highest earners among the self-employed. Only a minority of employees and of the self-employed are covered by private pension schemes yet all taxpayers have to pay higher taxes to support their pension saving and supplement their income in retirement.

The inequities of the private pension system ought to be addressed. In order to do so, policymakers would need to explore and resolve a wide range of issues including granting pension tax relief as a tax credit so that it has the same value for all taxpayers, phasing out the tax free lump sum so that all benefits are payable as a pension, establishing a relationship between the income cap on pension contributions and gross average earnings that would target the tax reliefs on middle and lower income groups, and introducing an annual tax on the returns on pension investments[7]. Sweden, Australia and New Zealand have all instituted major reforms of their tax arrangement for private pensions. Their experiences would provide a useful guide to resolving the administrative and practical problems that would arise in reforming the tax arrangements for private pensions in Ireland.

The significance of the inequitable tax arrangements for private pensions is considerable. As Hughes and Sinfield (2004) point out, there has been reluctance to improve State pension benefits because they will increase public expenditure but at the same time private pension provision is being actively encouraged although it reduces the tax revenue available for public expenditure. People are generally unaware of this because there is no annual review by the Dáil in which the cost of State support for the private pension system is compared with the cost of public expenditure on the State pension schemes. Only the cost of the State pension schemes receives any attention in the annual Dáil review of public expenditure. The result is that the argument over the increasing cost of pensions due to population ageing has been one sided with attention focussing only on the cost of the State pension schemes and the cost of tax reliefs for private pension schemes being ignored.

Notes

1   I am grateful to my colleague Bertrand Maitre for providing the data on pension coverage and pension tax reliefs by income decile.
2   The private pension system consists of occupational pension schemes (including Additional Voluntary Contributions) for private and public sector employees and Retirement Annuity Contracts for the self-employed and since 2003 Personal Retirement Savings Accounts for individuals. The public pension system, which is described more fully in the previous chapter, includes the State contributory and non-contributory pension schemes and the pension schemes for widows and widowers.
3   Structural tax reliefs are assumed to be part of the benchmark tax system.
4   The target is to increase coverage from 54 per cent of those aged 30-65 at work in 1995 to 66 percent in 2005 and to 70 per cent ultimately.
5   The pattern is similar when pension coverage rates are estimated by age group.
6   The distribution of the tax reliefs is derived separately for each group. Consequently the quintiles for each group do not refer to the same income classes.
7   The cap on the amount of salary or earnings on which individuals could make pension contributions allowable for tax relief was €254,000 in 2004.

References

Agulnik, P. and J. Le Grand (1998)," Tax Relief and Partnership Pensions", *Fiscal Studies*, Vol. 19, No. 4.

Commission on Taxation (1982), *First Report of the Commission on Taxation: Direct Taxation*, Dublin: Stationery Office (Pl. 617).

Commission on Taxation (1982), *First Report of the Commission on Taxation: Direct Taxation*, Dublin: Stationery Office (Pl. 617).

Department of Social Welfare (1976), *A National Income-Related Pension Scheme*, Dublin: Stationery Office, Pl: 5737.

Hughes, G. and B. Nolan (1999), "Competitive and Segmented Labour Markets and Exclusion from Retirement Income" in W. Salverda, B. Nolan, and C. Lucifora (eds) *Policy Measures for Low-Wage Employment in Europe*, Edward Elgar (forthcoming).

Hughes, G. and A. Sinfield (2004), "Financing Pensions by Stealth: The Anglo-American Model and the Cost and Distribution of Tax Benefits for Private Pensions" in G. Hughes and J. Stewart (eds.) *Reforming Pensions in Europe: Evolution of Pension Financing and Sources of Retirement Income*, Cheltenham: Edward Elgar.

Hughes, G. and D. Watson (2005), *Pensioners' Income and Replacement Rates in 2000*, Dublin: The Economic and Social Research Institute, Policy Research Series.

Irish Association of Pension Funds (1998), *Fact Sheet*, Dublin: Irish Association of Pension Funds (mimeo).

Irish Association of Pension Funds (1999), *Submission to Government Working Parties on the National Pensions Policy Initiative*, Dublin: Irish Association of Pension Funds (mimeo).

Keogh, G. and B. J. Whelan (1985), *National Survey of Occupational Pension Schemes*, Dublin: The Economic and Social Research Institute (mimeo).

National Pensions Board (1988), *Report on the Tax Treatment of Occupational Pension Scheme*, Dublin: Stationery Office.

Maitre, B. and B. Nolan (2001), Tax Progressivity and Pension Tax Expenditures in Ireland, Dublin: The Economic and Social Research Institute (mimeo).

Nolan, B., B. Gannon, R. Layte, D. Watson, C. T. Whelan and J. Williams (2002) *Monitoring Poverty Trends in Ireland: Results from the 2000 Living in Ireland* Survey, Dublin: The Economic and Social Research Institute, Policy Research Series No. 45.

OECD (1992), *Private Pensions and Public Policy*, Paris: Organisation for Economic Co-operation and Development.

Pensions Board (1997), *National Pensions Policy Initiative Consultation Document*, Dublin: The Pensions Board.

Pensions Board (1998), *Securing Retirement Income*, Dublin: The Pensions Board.

Sinfield, A. (1997), "Social Protection versus Tax Benefits" in European Institute of Social Security, *Social Protection of the Next Generation in Europe*, The Hague: Kluwer Law International.

Chapter 7

What Can Ireland Learn from the UK Experience?

BY SUE WARD

Note: Not long after this contribution was written, the First Report of the Pensions Commission *(Pensions: Challenges and Choices,* October 2004 – downloadable from www.pensionscommission.org. uk/index.asp) – was published. It is a formidable document with a wealth of statistical information, and I commend it to anyone trying to get to grips with the complexities of the UK situation.

7.1 INTRODUCTION

There is quite a tradition, this side of the water, of watching what we do on pensions, seeing where it goes wrong, and doing something else. So, for instance, Ireland never went down the road of having an additional State pension and then allowing people to contract-out of it – something which has cost the UK Exchequer a lot of money but is now unravelling before our eyes. Ireland launched PRSAs, the equivalent of our Personal Pensions, but did not provide the big sales-bribes out of public money that the UK Government did, and that led to a major misselling scandal in the 1990s. And hopefully, you are watching what's happening at the moment, with the massive extension of means-testing for pensioners, and a whole new raft of legislation, and deciding you could do better yourselves in those ways, too.

7.2 THE STATE PENSION SYSTEM

The first major flaw in the UK system is the level of the basic State pension. This is low, too low for anyone to live on without other money, and is increased only in line with prices – though currently underpinned with a promise of at least a 2.5 per cent annual increase during this Parliament – so that it is steadily falling relative to earnings. The single pension is now 16 per cent of National Average Earnings, and will be down to less than 10 per cent by 2029 (Pensions Policy Institute, 2004, p. 19).

The State pension is financed by National Insurance contributions, and the textbooks say it is universal, that is available to all those aged over 65, but it is in fact not universal. There is a complex system of credits and protections to cover periods when people are not earning for one reason or another. As a consequence, coverage is near universal for men, but getting towards it for women. However, because the various bits of the pension system were put in at different times, there are some internal contradictions and some rules that are convenient for the administrators but not for individuals, and as a consequence it is much easier than it should be to have gaps. Among other things, the system is organised in terms of tax years; if you moved, say, from childcare to a low-paid job at the New Year, you would probably lose that year as a contribution year in consequence. Because benefits are a function of the number of contribution years, State social insurance payments are reduced.

As a result of pressure from the Equal Opportunities Commission, the Government has promised not a change, but a report, on women and pensions, sometime next year. Meanwhile, though, an eminent committee of our House of Lords has suggested that esoteric tinkering with little obscure rules is a waste of time. Their proposal is simply to abolish all these contribution requirements, and make this a citizenship pension that is payable to all UK citizens. Many other people and organisations have supported this proposal, including the National Association of Pension Funds, which is working with researchers at the Pensions Policy Institute on the detail. There is a growing consensus that the low level and limitations of the State basic pension are at the roots of our pension problem. Unfortunately, it's not a consensus shared by the Government – a crucial gap.

On top of the basic State pension is a second, additional pension. This has been operating since 1978 and has been subject to constant tinkering – most recently in 2002 when the State Earnings Related Pension (SERPS), was re-named the Second State Pension (S2P), and tilted towards the lower-paid. The successive waves of change have left it exceedingly complex and not worth very much anyway.

When the Government first announced their reform package, they said that in 2006-2007, if their new Stakeholder pensions – roughly equivalent to the Irish Standard PRSAs – were a success, they would turn S2P into a flat-rate pension for those under 45. Stakeholders have not been a success in terms of sales to the previously unpensioned – the TUC recently calculated that only 2.6 per cent of the workforce is contributing, and many of those on top of an occupational pension (Trades Union Congress, 2004). But although the Government has remained silent on this second stage of S2P, they have not publicly dropped the idea, creating more uncertainty in people's minds.

The 'Big Idea' of this reform package was that over

time, the ratio of pensioners' income coming from State and non-State sources would switch from 60 per cent State, 40 per cent private to the opposite, 40 per cent State and 60 per cent private. Whether this seems sensible as a policy goal or not, it was promptly contradicted by another 'Big Idea', the new means-tested Pension Credit (PC). Essentially the Credit is two means-tested benefits wrapped into one. The first, the Guarantee element, is an old-fashioned and relatively straightforward arrangement to top up a pensioner's income to a minimum amount, modest for the younger and healthier, rather higher for the elderly and infirm. The second, the Savings Credit is, according to the Government, designed to "reward those who have modest savings" – that is, if you have a certain level of income above the State basic pension, you receive extra money but for every extra £1 of income you have, you get 40p less. It's all about relatively small sums of money; the maximum weekly amount of Savings Credit is £15.51 for a single person, £20.22 for a couple (Pensions Policy Institute, 2004, p. 4), but around half the pensioner population is theoretically entitled to one or both elements. Since the PC limits are expected to rise in line with earnings rather than prices, it will in due course draw in around 80 per cent of the population – in theory, since the unsolved difficulty with means-tested benefits is that people do not claim. There were large claims by the Department for Work and Pensions (DWP) that "it would all be different this time, it's not like old means tests". Although the DWP, to their credit, had plans to go out and look for potential claimants, rather than just wait until people turned up. These plans have been set back – and it is a recurrent pattern whenever our Government revamps its social security arrangements – by the Treasury's decision to cut 30,000 civil servants from the DWP, so that offices that only opened a year ago are now being closed.

Even with around one-third of those eligible not

claiming, the Pension Credit is not cheap, and the Treasury uses some accounting sleight of hand to disguise how over-budget its spending projections now are. But it also affects the Government's plans in another way, because of the disincentive effects on saving. The Treasury simply refuses to accept these disincentive effects exist, in public at least. However, the rational person on whom their economic theory relies in general, given the alternatives of meeting current consumption needs which are certain, as opposed to making future gains which will probably be taken away, would definitely choose the first alternative. Too few people probably understand the detail to be positively put off saving, but it has an important "miasma" effect – and it also certainly means that financial advisers are very reluctant to give positive advice to lower-paid people about long-term savings. Financial advisers, in particular, experienced financial loss as a result of the UK's personal pensions misselling scandal. It provides a very good reason for not dealing with a group who are going to give the financial advisers a low financial gain anyway. Why not concentrate on the easy option of the high-net-worth individual?

The UK Government itself is planning to get round this problem by ignoring it! They have a quite sensible set of ideas called their "Informed Choice" agenda – things like issuing annual benefit statements for State pensions, automatically – and one of them is that they are going to have a "web-based retirement planner", so you can see how much, based on their assumptions, you should have saved each month (Department of Work and Pensions, 2004). The pilot version of this scheme reported to the House of Lords made no mention at all of the Pension Credit (House of Lords, 2004). (When I personally contacted the DWP about it, they said that this was the sort of detail that would be worked on in piloting exercises).

7.3 OCCUPATIONAL PENSIONS

Meanwhile, outside the unfunded public sector schemes, occupational pensions are in a sorry state, with large deficits following a number of years of large surpluses. After the Maxwell debacle in 1991, the Goode Committee on Pension Law Reform (Pension Law Review Committee, 1993, on which I sat), proposed that pension schemes should have a Minimum Solvency Requirement which was going to be fairly tough – though probably not enough to withstand the current crisis. This got watered down into the Minimum Funding Requirement (MFR) before it came into force in 1997, and had to be altered shortly afterwards when the Chancellor, Gordon Brown, altered pension funds' tax position. This solvency standard did not work very well because of its methodology at the time when the stock market was at an all-time high. Unfortunately, it did not work any better, in terms of protecting pensions, after the stock market crash. A scheme can be 100 per cent funded on the MFR (not that many are, at present) and still not have enough money to pay full benefits when it is discontinued. Until June last year, solvent employers could walk away from the pension scheme and only have to pay the MFR deficit. That gap is now largely closed, but with the resounding clatter of stable doors being closed after the horse has bolted!

As a result, people are increasingly being asked to rely on employers' pensions that are built on sand. The only way someone can be sure that their past benefits in the scheme are safe, is if the scheme is funded at all times for full benefits on discontinuance, including the costs of buying those benefits. The funds must then be invested in low risk and hence low return assets. The only way they can be sure of security for the benefits they are promised in the future, is if they know that enough contributions are going in for the benefits to be paid, *even if* all the contributions are invested in risk-free, and hence low-return, investments. In essence, what our current funding techniques and investment methods do, are assume that you can have the return due on risky investments like equities, without carrying the risk. That is economic nonsense.

If giving benefit security is impossibly expensive for employers, as they claim, then should they be promising or should they ever have promised such benefits? And should the Government be relying on those promises for the living standards of its elderly citizens?

The Government is now planning to supersede the Minimum Funding Requirement with a "scheme-specific funding standard" (SSFS) – though so far there are only rather sketchy details of what this will do. It appears to rely on the fact that if you are a good strong employer with a healthy balance sheet, the trustees can take a risk, if the pension scheme is currently under-funded, that the pension scheme will eventually be fully funded, compared with an employer that is financially weak. Leaving aside the fact that an employer can look strong one day and appear insolvent within a short time – as with GEC/Marconi or Enron. One implication is that at just the point when creditors (for example, banks) are insisting on extra guarantees and loan repayments, the pension fund trustees are supposed to put a large bill for extra contributions on the employer's desk as well. I think the SSFS is a retrograde step and will be reformed again in a few years – unless the actuaries have the courage to insist that it means full discontinuance funding for any employer that is remotely insecure.

The same Pensions Act (2004),also brings in a Pension Protection Fund (PPF), and alongside it a Financial Assistance Scheme, for the 60,000 people without pension coverage due to closure of the place of employment, changes in pension scheme rules, etc. before the Act was introduced. I have always felt that the idea of each employer running their own little pension scheme, without mutual insurance to back it up, was a nonsense, "like a community denying itself a fire brigade", as one critic, John Shuttleworth has put it. But bringing in the PPF now, with occupational pension schemes in such poor state, could be unworkable – especially as it is being rushed in, with many of the details left for sorting out later. That includes, for instance, how the levy on pension funds will be related to risk. For example for the first year, perhaps longer, the levy will consist of a flat-rate element and will not vary with risk. It is not going to provide full benefits, but a "rough justice" standard package, with very little by way of pension increases. The cost of that package, on discontinuance, will probably become the *ad hoc* funding standard for all schemes.

The PPF is modelled on the Pension Benefit Guaranty Corporation in the US, which may itself be in serious difficulty if the US Airlines liabilities fall on it. The same may happen to the PPF. It could survive even a couple of major bankruptcies in the first few years, because this is a slow fuse; to start with it could simply pay benefits out of the funds, on a pay-as-you-go basis. But gradually, the cash flow out could become larger than the inflow. The Government has said it will not bail out the PPF; it must raise the levy or cut the benefits. Any of those options would be pretty disastrous for people's faith in occupational pensions. While we wish the PPF well, building an avalanche fence when the avalanche is already running tends to result in a rather shaky fence.

There are calls, not least by our TUC, to fill the gap in the UK's pension provision by making it compulsory for employers and employees to pay into a pension scheme – whether an occupational or a personal one. My own view is that without much stronger foundations, that would be immoral – and politically impossible as well. Could you require people to pay into a pension scheme that was already in deficit and where the employer was struggling?

Hardly, without the Government underwriting all liabilities. Could you require low-paid people, who were never going to get above the Pension Credit's basic level, to pay out money now for no gain later? I doubt it.

Finally, as part of the upheaval that is going on in the UK pensions system at present, we have "tax simplification" – though simplifying does seem to have got very complicated. To give the basic picture, all our rules about the maximum occupational pension or the maximum contributions related to earnings are being swept away from April 2006. Instead, there will be a "lifetime allowance" of a £1.5m capital sum, which on a rough-and-ready 20:1 formula is calculated to be enough to provide a £75,000 pension. You can have more if you want, but you pay tax on it. Anyone can have up to 25 per cent of their fund in tax-free cash at the time they retire, which is going to give most people much more than they can have at present. Up to 100 per cent of your earnings can go into your pension fund in any one year, assuming you can afford that. There are some elaborate transitional arrangements for that very small group of the population who may be disadvantaged by the limits – at the outside 100,000 people, less than 0.5 per cent of the working population.

That small group, however, have been mounting a ferocious lobbying campaign to keep their current privileges and have enlisted most of the pensions industry's consultant expertise to assist them. The top people in the pensions industry, of course, are sufficiently highly paid to belong to that elite themselves, and of course they are aware who pays their bill. The Treasury has given some fairly significant concessions, believing them to be a price worth paying to achieve simplification, and has got through with its main principles unscathed. But it is a sign of the difficulties any Government faces when making radical changes in pensions.

7.4 CONCLUSION

To summarise the lessons to be drawn from the UK experience:

The level, and the coverage, of the basic State pension is key. A citizenship pension that provides a realistic amount to live on can act as the foundation for everything else. Without it, the other elements are shaky indeed.

One reason the UK's State pension has been able to fall so low is that it has not been clear to people what is happening, so transparency and simplicity in pension systems are also important.

Everyone, except the Government, believes that the steps towards near-universal means-testing for pensioners are a mistake, but reversing the policy is difficult and expensive; and the longer means-testing exists, the more difficult it will be to change. Pensions policy is highly path-dependent; once you start down one track, it is hard to go back. Change needs to be properly thought out and researched, and real efforts made to reach a consensus.

Pensions involve thinking ahead – much further than the lifetime of one government – which is another reason for trying to seek a consensus. The time for putting in proper safeguards is when things are going well, not when they are already going wrong.

It is, it seems, too expensive for employers to provide properly secure pensions that their ex-workers can rely on in retirement. If that's the case, they should not be made to rely on them. If you have only risky varieties of private pensions, they should just serve the function of topping up an existing pension – the icing on the cake. Conversely, if private pensions are to form the basis of pension income – 'the bread and butter' – then they must be made properly secure, whether by full funding, by mutual insurance, or by a government guarantee.

The resources to provide decent pensions for everyone

are clearly there in the UK, but are unevenly and wastefully distributed. Our Liberal Democrats, for example, have proposed financing changes to the State pension system, such as increased pensions and introducing a 'citizens pensions' by raising an estimated Stg 5.2 bn from higher rate tax payers (Liberal Democrats, 2005 Policy Briefing 8 and Institute for Fiscal Studies Press release 28 February 2005). But as we have seen in the tax simplification saga, and my final lesson from UK experience: When you try to make changes, those who are privileged by the current system will fight ferociously (and effectively) to maintain their privileges.

References

Department for Work and Pensions (2004), *Simplicity, security and choice: Informed choices for working and saving*, London: Department for Work and Pensions.

House of Lords Hansard, 10 June 2004, col. 244

Pension Law Review Committee, *Pension Law Reform: the Report of the Pension Law Review Committee*, London: HMSO, 1993.

Pensions Policy Institute (2004), *Pensions Primer*, London: Pensions Policy Institute.

Trades Union Congress, 'Tax dodge' stakeholders hide workers' low contributions' TUC press release, 10 August 2004.

SOME COMMONLY USED TERMS*

Actuarial Deficit – the pension payments calculated by an actuary are greater than the assets of the pension scheme.

Additional Voluntary Contribution (AVC) – extra contributions that may be made to increase eventual pension payments. AVC schemes are often organised separately from the main pension scheme.

Annuity – a series of payments made in return for a fixed payment. In pension schemes, payments are for life and, depending on the annuity contract, may increase with the rate of inflation or general pay levels.

Contributory Pension – a pension scheme that requires contributions. In the case of the State pension scheme, contributions and payment levels are determined by the Department of Social and Family Affairs.

Defined Benefit Scheme – pension benefits are stated in scheme rules and are in general some fraction of final salary, for example a half or two-thirds.

Defined Contribution Scheme – a pension scheme where contributions by employer and employee are fixed and where pension payments are determined by the value of contributions and the rate of return.

Funded Pension – a pension which is provided from assets that are held and managed separately from the employer.

Funding Standard – a requirement that defined benefit schemes have enough assets to meet liabilities.

Irish Financial Services Regulatory Authority (IFSRA) – regulates all financial services firms in Ireland.

Non-Contributory Pension – a pension scheme that does not require contributions. In general, this refers to the State non-contributory pension which is means-tested.

Pay-as-you-go pension – pensions that are financed out of current income or taxation in the case of pensions from the State.

Pensions Board – a statutory body which regulates pensions and advises the Government on pension matters.

Personal Retirement Savings Account (PRSA) – individual pensions savings plan which benefits from tax reliefs. Employers may contribute as well as employees, but in general do not do so.

Special Savings Investment Accounts (SSIA) – a type of savings account (now ended) that required monthly payments into a savings or investment account, over a five-year period. The State contributed a further 25 per cent in addition to any investment returns or interest earned.

Tax Expenditure – the cost of a tax relief in terms of taxes not paid.

* For a comprehensive definition of other terms used in pension issues see *Commission on Public Sector Pensions,* glossary of terms used, available at www.finance.gov.ie. See also *Pensions Board, So You' re a Pension Scheme Trustee?*, and other publications available at www.pensions-board.ie.

Index